ETHICAL DILEMMAS

CRISES IN FAITH AND MODERN MEDICINE

Edited by

JOHN T. CHIRBAN

UNIVERSITY
PRESS OF
AMERICA

Lanham • New York • London

Copyright © 1994 by
University Press of America®, Inc.
4720 Boston Way
Lanham, Maryland 20706

3 Henrietta Street
London WC2E 8LU England

Library of Congress Cataloging-in-Publication Data

Ethical dilemmas : crises in faith and modern medicine /
edited by John T. Chirban.
p.   cm.
Includes bibliographical references.
1. Medical ethics.   2. Christian ethics.   I. Chirban, John T.
R724.E785   1994   174'.2—dc20   93–34746 CIP

ISBN 0–8191–9337–2 (cloth : alk. paper)
ISBN 0–8191–9338–0 (pbk. : alk. paper)

Contents

Introduction

Technological advances have ushered in a flood of questions for which modern society has not been able to judge what is "right" and what is "wrong." Furthermore, our views on issues for which we thought "we have the answers" have had to be revisited because of how medical advances have changed our understanding of life itself.

Approaching medical ethical problems is a task for both science and religion. Although it may well be that scientific advances generate the questions, it is only out of particular traditions that beliefs and values are born and breathe. This book turns to science and to faith, to theory and to human experience, to specialists of body, mind, and soul, in an effort to present a wholistic approach to problems in medical ethics.

Ethical Dilemmas: Crises in Faith and Modern Medicine presents five controversial issues that stir moral conflicts in our time: bioethics, euthanasia, decisions near death, bio-engineering and genetic engineering and substance abuse. These topics are examined from interdisciplinary perspectives. They reflect the expertise of physicians, mental health professionals, and theologians who presented their views at the Sixth National Conference of the Orthodox Christian Association of Medicine, Psychology and Religion.

Their presentations show how religious beliefs come to bear on clinical situations and interventions; how *theoria*, theory, informs *praxis*, practice. This collection of articles does not offer dogmatic treatment of contemporary problems but identifies some of the difficulties of applying traditional values to modern medical concerns, and articulates and develops how traditional perspectives provide the needed rudder in addressing modern ethical problems.

These papers reflect an interdisciplinary approach which expresses sensitivity and appreciation of multiple perspectives of contemporary human problems. The discussions in this volume present a laboratory of investigation, showing how important it is to appreciate the role of the sacred upon modern technology and clinical services.

Dr. Martin Marty, professor of religion at the University of Chicago, places the volume into historical perspective with his prologue, "The Ethical Challenges of Science." Dr. Marty discusses the difficulties in the dialogue between religion and science and the necessity for communication between the fields. He observes that in modern times science turns to faith for direction, and he concludes that faithful communities must rediscover their identities to help respond to modern dilemmas.

The ethical topic of euthanasia is presented by four professors. Dr. William F. May, professor of ethics at Southern Methodist University, addresses the subject, "Changing Conceptions of a Good Death: Its Bearing on the Physician's Words and Deeds." This article provides an overview of the debate concerning euthanasia. Dr. Vigen Guroian, professor of religion at Loyola College, appeals to an understanding of "good" death and dying based upon Patristic literature and contemporary ethical thinkers. Rev. Dr. John Breck, professor of New Testament and ethics at St. Vladimir's Seminary, argues that euthanasia must be rejected because of "the problems" associated with assuming responsibility for the decisions of life and death and explains other "options" besides euthanasia. Finally, Dr. John Demakis, professor of clinical medicine at Loyola University's Stritch School of Medicine, demonstrates how faith and science meet in his paper, "Euthanasia: The Medical Encounter and Faith."

In discussing concerns and decisions near the end of life, Monk Ioannikios and several physicians offer guidelines about the appropriateness and design of a living will. In the controversial matter of organ transplants, Dr. Sharon Chirban, a clinical fellow in psychology at Harvard Medical School at The Cambridge Hospital, explains the ethical concerns and appropriate management of organ transplants.

The subject of genetic and bio-engineering is discussed in terms of its scientific and theological impact by Dr. Demetrios Demopulos, a geneticist from the University of Wisconsin and candidate for priesthood, and Dr. Frank Papatheofanis, a physician and professor of bio-engineering at the University of Illinois, from the perspective of genetic engineering and bio-mechanical engineering, respectively. Here, theology is brought into focus by scientists who consider applications of engineering into human life.

Substance abuse is the final topic considered. In my presentation, "Drugs and the Family," the antidote for drug abuse is examined not only in terms of biology and psychology but also in terms of spirituality. Lyn Breck, a substance abuse counselor, discusses the management of addiction and the role of the church in her paper, "Towards a Recovery-Oriented Church." And, finally, the problem of addiction is brought together with ethics by James Campbell, a student of theology from the University of Chicago, who correlates "usury" and drugs to the problem of "taking responsibility."

I wish to acknowledge Ms. Sophia Apessos, who diligently prepared this manuscript for publication. I am thankful for her steady ways and computer dexterity.

John T. Chirban
Lexington, Massachusetts

PART I

Bioethics

The field that addresses new questions about life and moral judgements concerning medical advances is "bioethics." The very definitions of when life begins and ends have been challenged because of the ways in which medical technology contributes to modern society. How do we know when conception begins? Do understandings of contraception interfere with human life? At what point does death occur? When there are no brain waves? If the heart ceases to beat? When do we draw the line for maintaining extraordinary technology to sustain life processes?

These are some of the basic issues to which leaders in medicine, psychology and religion respond in this volume. Professor Martin Marty sets the stage for the requisite dialogue of science and faith, identifying the complexity of this task while defending the interdependence of these fields for responding to ethical dilemmas of our time.

The Ethical Challenges of Science and Faith

Martin Marty

There is a good reminder of how young the discipline of bioethics is. It has roots in Ancient Greece, in the people of God in Israel of old, and in early Christianity. Bioethics has a long history of philosophy, yet modern medical ethics is by definition a very recent formation.

I have been reading in order to write an introduction to a book about nine middle generation ethicists writing about nine senior ethicists. Two celebrated names include Professor Paul Ramsey, who has had a considerable influence on one of our presenters, William May, and Professor Joseph Fletcher, who began writing about ethics in the middle of the 1950's. Fletcher's book of 1954, *Morals and Medicine*, is often taken as a measure of the history of theology and medicine. We always have difficulty when bringing people together embodied in a group like the Orthodox Christian Association of Medicine, Psychology and Religion (OCAMPR), primarily because we are bringing together two contrasting groups: people in the world of medicine and medical science, on the one hand, and those in ethics and theology, on the other. As George Steiner reminds us, medicine and science mainly look forward. Science likes to trash its own past.

A child in second and third grade probably can do some things towards which Euclid, Galen and Pythagoras spent their lives working. In the humanities from which we draw ethics, philosophy, and theology, we look backward.

George Steiner reminds us that there is probably not a new Plato sitting among the philosophers of our generation, that no dramatist is likely to exceed Shakespeare in depth and scope, and that none of the finest composers of our day will outdo Mozart; so, like Janus, we look forward and backward all the time. But one of the things we are learning is that medicine, and likewise science, situates itself in humanistic and theological traditions. It makes statements through actualization about long traditions and medical ethics and projects them from the present into the future.

Not long after World War II, I recall reading in a national magazine how the United States government was helping to rebuild German universities. The American team asked a professor of chemistry, who was leading them around, "All right, we see how these two hundred million dollars are going into laboratories and clinics, but what about that very famous philosophy and theology school?" The chemist replied, "Oh, the theologians will never discover anything new over there." As far as he was concerned, ancient texts lay there as a repository of the human story, similar to museums and antique shops.

What interested me in the nine essays about the recent past and contemporary ethicists is how they take the ancient word and apply it to unforeseen modern situations. I graduated from theological school in 1952 and received my doctorate in history in 1956. I believe that when we try to envision the themes of medicine, psychology, and psychiatry, everything that is typical today was science fiction then. Today a physician, a nurse, a counselor or a priest confronts ever week something that may have looked like fantasy in the past. The traditional tests are renewed in this encounter and that is part of the excitement. For this reason I think people far beyond Orthodoxy will be interested in what OCAMPR is addressing so formally in ethics.

When modern medical ethics was formulated it was founded in theology, then was eclipsed, but is now returning. When Roman Catholics, Orthodox, Protestant Traditionalists, and Jews assert a theological viewpoint, it is startlingly fresh to people in clinical ethics and universities.

Assertion in such an environment is never done without some measure of abrasion, difficulty, and maybe even shock. I hope some shock is involved, because nobody, nor any one tradition, has the field to itself. We are a society defining itself as pluralistic, a way of saying we are highly diverse and have ground rules for these diverse elements to communicate. "Any number can play," to use atheistic or card-table terms. Any number can play, great numbers do, and there are established rules of the game. When religious and theological voices are reintroduced to medical ethics, some of the rules are pushed to the edges. This is what makes it so interesting now. Most of the discourse about medical ethics in our time derives from Greek or Roman and Hebrew-Christian sources, the two great fonts of our tradition, and are filtered and transmuted through renaissances and enlightenments. Through their solidarity people still struggle over these changes. For a lot of people these discourses are old, remote, and every day more distant; the stories are harder to hear and to understand; the symbols less accessible.

Twenty and thirty years ago, it was harder to talk about faith looking forward. A lot of people said, "These traditions mean nothing to us; we'll trample them and leave them behind." Professor Goodheart, a reasonable radical, spoke to them at the time and said of the Greek or Roman and the Hebrew-Christian traditions: "Be not possessed with traditions. Let the traditions possess you." So much of our life is gestural, inherited, reflexive, and only semi-conscious. The way words, terms, and symbols were used; all were medicine in ancient times.

Think of how much of Greek mythology we captured. Through many centuries, how much of the language of care is born from religious orders, including monks, nuns, and healers of Eastern and Western Europe alike. Modernity, in Anthony Given's terms, is a disembedding phenomenon. Things are embedded in tradition, plants are embedded in soil; yet modernity uproots and transplants, disembedding elements from tradition and fusing them with advances in science. Orthodoxy is one among Christian voices, one among many voices. A survey of one hundred thirty-three thousand Americans last year lists eighty-five percent of the America people identifying themselves with Christianity in the broadest sense. Yet Christianity itself remains an alien voice in discussions of our culture.

We are pluralists in many ways. We are pluralists concerning gender. Women reread ancient texts and interpret in the light of their experience, and gain a different meaning. Liberal and conservative cultures are deeply anchored in our histories, so that the contemporary dilemmas facing the family or education, for example, are more culturally-based than politically-generated.

My family is not your family, my tribe not your tribe; I am Swiss and I come with two watches and you are Greek, you come when you get here. We adopted two Hispanic children and got used to the Hispanic culture and I thought they had a monopoly on coming "when you get here." It is a very different thing to be in a Swiss culture, being compulsive and Protestant, than in a somewhat more relaxed tempo and in a different culture.

It is very poignant, powerful and disconcerting to look at tens of millions of people today in certain economic groups, or ethnic groups such as Hispanics or African-Americans, who may have an experience of being excluded, for example, where medical resources are allocated. It is very different to read about those situations and traditions, or to read Gospels about the message of God in Christ to the oppressed and to have a very vivid sense of inheritance of slavery or segregation. We are pluralists in our philosophies. When I say Plato and Aristotle, I am not talking about one thing, though they may be near contemporaries and both Greek. There is a great canyon running through our culture depending on which of these camps one finds more congenial. Among Kant, Hegel, Russell, Liechtenstein, and Dully, most Americans do not know whether they are pragmatists or idealists, but if you listen to them, you will know who is monistic and who is dualistic. People need commitments about the meaning of the body, the good, care, and justice in light of these philosophies. OCAMPR consists of all those parts. This organization is perceived most of all as representing a religious element inside pluralism-- indeed, within organized religion.

Everybody in America wants to be known as religious or spiritual these days, but in organized religion, people;e are responsible in "ecclesia" to each other, to a Word, to the sacramental life. People have bishops and presbyters, congregations and parishes, dioceses and denominations, representing walled institutions to the larger culture. When views are asserted from inside, it puzzles the rest of the culture.

In the midst of all that is the tradition of modern medical ethics, which is friendly to religion without integrating its insights into all the discourse at universities or clinical ethics departments at teaching hospitals. There, the Hebrew-Christian tradition is suppressed in favor of the Greco-Roman tradition filtered through the Western enlightenment, the tradition that shapes everybody. It creates the envelope which we are, the air we breathe. My former colleague, Langden Gillckie, says of the secular rational culture around us that we are to it as the Greeks were to Hellenism. I doubt, for example, that one could awaken a Greek back then and ask, "What are you?" and hear the response: "I am a Hellenist." We defined them as that a good deal later. So now we define our secular rationality or a liberal culture as the environment around us. This is assumed to be the basis of language about medical ethics.

Robert Booth Fowler, professor of political science at the University of Wisconsin, has tried to define our culture as a "liberal culture." Not liberal in the sense of the big "L" of the Democratic party or the big "L" of the University of Chicago economics department, that is, liberal in the sense of political left and right. Instead, Fowler's liberal has three features: First, we instinctively move on the basis of secular rationality. We do not introduce the theological question to initiate a discourse. This becomes very clear in a medical situation. If I am going in for neural surgery, I would be quite disconcerted if the neural surgeon said, "I don't know much about neural surgery, but I am a very intense Mormon." Or if the anesthesiologist said, "Well, you're going to get a Baptist anesthesiology today but I am not very good at reading the meters." We want our medicine to be grounded i certain assumptions about reality, to be purely identifiable, tested in the laboratory, and transferred into all the dimensions of life.

The second feature of a liberal culture, which we breathe just by living here now, is characterized by a religious tolerance bordering on indifference, which is our way of saying we like religions to be present, but it is a private affair. One of my employers, Jim Wall, editor of the *Christian Century*, was the Illinois chair for Jimmy Carter's presidential campaign. Everyone knew that Mr. Carter was very religious. When NBC asked him if he had a personal experience with Jesus, he told them he was "born again." This absolutely befuddled NBC, having never met anybody who had been "born again," although the vast majority of Americans had. I always told Mr. Wall that in their campaign they were doing two very interesting things with Mr. Carter. First, they were telling the American people the benefits of his religiousness, but also that Carter's religiousness would not affect his job performance. NBC was worried about what would happen if particulars entered into the general discourse; religion is nice but don't bring it up in a clinic.

The third feature in a liberal culture, according to Robert Booth Fowler, is "extreme individualism." I have emphasized organized church, as institution, as *ecclesia*, as body, because that is how it gets social or communal quality, just an interesting idiosyncratic element in the life of the biography of people in *Who's Who*. When they band together, they are mutually covenanted, and are responsive in a tradition to texts, to each other, and to causes; they bump into each other. They push at the edges of the boundaries of the secular rational, which are indifference, and extreme individualism. Fowler says that the interesting thing about the moment in which we find ourselves today is that while we keep living with those three impacts of liberal culture we have found them spiritually unsatisfying. They are marvelous for the functioning of a culture, but they tell us very little about the passages of life: about what hits you at three in the morning when you awaken and think of birth and death, the small scope of human life and the vastness of eternity. We do not care a great deal about secular rationality and tolerance bordering on indifference and extreme individualism: At those moments you ask a different set of questions.

We are not going to demolish the marks of a liberal culture, but instead help people to tolerate and make way for questions that have not been heard. As far as secular rationality is concerned, most ethical language in our time revolves around just a few them in the major textbooks in medical schools.

Now I should say some good things in praise of human language. First of all, it is a tradition, and that is very helpful. That is, you can isolate it, define it, criticize it, and profit form it. You do not have to start form scratch every day wondering where "someone is coming from." They are coming from this body of ethical language. Language is an aid to efficiency because it is a reflexive element in the culture. I think it is good because it aspires to speak universally and generically. In effect, it says we do not care if you are a Jehovahs Witness or Seventh Day Adventist or whatever. If you think deeply about these things, you will agree. Autonomy, justice, melephasis, and non-melephasis are keystones for any thinking people.

It is in the tradition of the enlightenment of the West and the founding of America that claims are to be based entirely on reason and do not depend on revelation. James Madison reminded us that it would be hard to get a republic going if everyone had a revelation form God, and then tried to enact that message into the law of the land. Among the vast majority of the population are people who do not agree with us religiously. We would have to impose the revelation on them. (And that sort of matches the ethos of military culture).

In my own reading in medical ethics, I am influenced by Kent Greenwald's reminder of the way we actually make decisions. Mark Seigler, chairman of clinical ethics at the University of Chicago, who is more critical than I would be of the academic philosophy, but who leaves a lot of room for the religious voice, says when you are involved in a crisis, like euthanasia or genetic engineering, you do not invite the academic philosopher in to give a lecture on Aristotle's view of ethics. You ask, "What does my good doctor say? What does my pastor or my priest say? What does my family say?" This may very well be code language for considering what God would say.

Many things come close to the language of the church. We reason about our own ethical situations and confrontations in the light of memory. If the Orthodox start forgiving, then we are all in trouble. Community: How does this body of people do it? Hope, intuition, affection or affectivity-- we have common experiences and we have to act upon them. I do not think Greenwald believes that religious language can become the language of simple legislation, or the language of the philosophy department, or the language of the clinic. Nothing is simple in our culture, and I am not trying to describe it that way. Rather, I am saying that the return of religious voices to medical ethics adds complications. They make it more complex because they try to bring in the real lives of people. When the academic talks to the academic a certain language is used. Think of the patients as the fixed points of all your deliberations. Think of the world the patient brings-- the world of family, religion, learning, and experience.

There is a realization of the complexity of philosophy of secular rationalism, tolerance bordering on indifference and extreme individualism going on within this philosophy itself. People like Liechtenstein have begun to ask questions about language philosophy. Scientific philosophers like Thomas Coon and Michael Polony have pushed it further. It is being questioned from within because of its exposure, and because of its foreign "otherness," to other cultures. We bump into the way that the Japanese do it, because they do not think in terms of Aristotle and Kant. Yet there are a lot of good medics and ethical people there. African clinics and the Christian missions find themselves running into cultures in Africa that think quite differently after a century or two of exposure to Western technology.   Behind the militancy of local tradition, people say, "Don't speak for me," when they think you are talking the universal language.

I think the great aid that can come from religious and theological voices is "complexifying," the thickening of it all.   Religious traditions are thick, involving people, memory, community, hope, intuition, affection, and experience. How do we do this? By speaking to the mainstream, we will make more vivid our awareness of the importance of the people involved. By listening to the tradition, to the people, and the priest who lives between text and people. Listen to each other: the secular rationalist, the Japanese, the Africans, the Aristotelians, the Orthodox Jews, and the Methodists do listen to each other.   Congregation always produces the risk of change through professional inquiry; we have institutes for the study of religious languages.   We have the words of the various traditions.   Even legislatures cannot write laws without the voice of religion being brought in. Legislatures will always make an issue more complex.

I suggested that it was harder to talk about religion and theology twenty or thirty years ago than it is now. Today, some of the luster is removed from the image of the purely secular. There has been an equally paradoxical increase of religious interest in the culture that calls itself secular. The vividness of religious experience twenty and thirty years ago, the language of addiction, the spirituality of the twelve steps of Alcoholics Anonymous, were all hidden secrets. Now those languages are very open and public. the language of incest and abuse was not heard as vividly then as it is now. Now when people speak up for themselves as victims, as healers, they find themselves drawing upon the resources of faith more than any of the other alternatives.

To conclude, I am not assuming that the culture is going to stop being a liberal culture. In a sense, Fowler says we maintain our faiths, our religions, and our churches and then retreat from them. The we repeat the cycle and go back into it. I think that is what is going to happen. Our culture takes on a different character when we come back into it. Stimulating the conversation by being articulate about what each tradition contributes is important. We also need to ask what is in our traditions as we meet the others; what stands behind the kind of language we have.

I do not think we are labeling the conversation in order to turn sectarian and to build walls between people. We can still aspire to common interest in human family not matter what gender, philosophy, culture, race or religion we might claim. We are aware of the limits in a republic; we cannot win them all. There are times when the courts will intervene and give a blood transfusion to a Jehovah's Witness child against the theology of the people. For the most part, we can see such debates as a positive thickening of the understanding of language.

What is expected of professionals in this kind of world? Obviously you can't be encyclopedic about it all. There is no way that somebody who is Orthodox can pretend to know the nuances of Orthodox Judaism. It takes a lifetime to learn the languages of the texts. We do not pretend that we can learn them all. We are open to the voices of the articulators of those traditions, and we interpret circumstances that reflect on our own so that we can better share it with each other. It is in that spirit that I have been privileged to address you this day of the inauguration of your Ethics Institute.

Reference

Fletcher, Joseph (1954). *Morals and Medicine.* Princeton, New Jersey: Princeton University Press.

PART II

Euthanasia

Twenty-one year old Karen Ann Quinlan ceased breathing on April 15, 1975 for unknown reasons. Although hospitalized and placed on a respirator, treatment was successful for restoring active life for Karen. She lied in bed alive but continuously comatose. Not until June 11, 1985, after the Supreme Court of New Jersey granted her father permission to turn off the respirator, did Karen die.

Biomedical advances have made this extraordinary-sounding case problem concerning euthanasia all too common in hospital settings. Before technological advances, most were resigned to the fate of "letting nature take its course." Today we have the means to intervene. Should we? If so, to what extent should we go to enable life to continue?

In this section, Professor William May discusses "good dying" as a problem for modern society, given our technological advances. He offers recommendations for how we may more effectively respond to dying in terms of active and passive euthanasia, identifying health care and hospital policies for: 1) maximal treatment and hospital care; 2) starting and stopping medicines; 3) ordinary and extraordinary means, and 4) allowing someone to die and mercy killing.

Professor Vigen Guroian explains the error of euthanasia from an Orthodox Christian perspective, based upon the Scriptures and pastoral theology. He offers practical applications of ethics and theology in conjunction with a case study.

Dr. John Breck examines the controversial side of physician-assisted suicide. He carefully discusses the merit of action (direct euthanasia) and the domain of passive euthanasia and identifies an agenda of issues for the "next steps in the debate."

Dr. John Demakis provides a case study that demonstrates the dilemmas for the Orthodox Christian physician concerning euthanasia. Dr. Demakis then analyzes passive euthanasia, active euthanasia, and the role of the Church and active euthanasia.

Changing Conceptions of a Good Death: Its Bearing on the Physician's Words and Deeds

William F. May

An ethics for living must ask the question: what is a good life? An ethics for dying must ask: what is a good death? Clearly, Western society has experienced a change in its conception of a good death.

I have asked audiences at the beginning of a speech what they consider to be a good death. "How would they like to go?" The answers, of course, vary, but inevitably, members of the audience mention two desires: They would like to go quickly, and with a minimum of pain and suffering.

We need not explain the desire to avoid pain and suffering, certainly not in a culture that aspires to an ever-richer quality of life. America clearly justifies its educational system as a means to enrich one's quality of life. Scientific knowledge and the technology that flows from it will lengthen life and enhance life's quality. Through education, students will acquire a professional identity and career that will expand their personal opportunities. Education provides the gateway to escape from limited life and misery. We so take that goal for granted that we forget that education, traditionally in the West, did not supply men and women with the means to eliminate or reduce suffering. Consider Greek tragedies, wherein the characters hoped simply to acquire a little wisdom in the midst of suffering.

Most modern people not only want a death free of suffering, they also want to go quickly. They prefer a heart attack to cancer. The sudden attack will let them avoid dying; they do not want to suffer dying. They would rather go quickly from living to dead.

A bar in Denver, Colorado, "Duffy's Shamrock," once displayed a poem above its cabinets full of liquor and beer that offered the following toast:

> Here's to a long life
> And a merry one
> A quick death and an easy one
> A pretty girl and a true one
> A cold beer and another one.

The poem expressed "Duffy's Credo" and the feelings of a lot of Americans.

Soren Kierkegaard, the 19th century Danish thinker, drew attention to the modern preference for a sudden death in his *Thoughts on Crucial Situations in Life.* Ironically, the 20th century has witnessed a preference for a sudden death, yet has produced incredibly expensive diagnostic tools (i.e., the so-called C-T Scanner, etc.), which serve as early warning systems about diseases, many of which are irremediable. The doctor juggles this very "hot" information. He could supply an early warning, but he also feels that his patients do not want it.

Why do people prefer a quick death? Generally, people want a warning in life to help them prepare for an event. This identical link between warning and preparation appears in the traditional prayers of the Christian Church. The believer, on "Rogation Day," prays for deliverance from a long list of evils--including war, floods, famine, and pestilence--but also the evil of a sudden and unprovided-for (that is, unprepared-for) death. Conversely, a good death includes a warning and very specific preparations.

In what follows, I draw heavily on Philippe Aries' account of the Western medieval sense of a good death, though, I believe, I could have appealed to other traditional societies. Medieval literature was filled with premonitions of death (Aries, 1971). The customary phrase was "his time has come." After forewarning, the dying man or woman prepared for death. First, the dying person might adopt prescribed gestures or postures: sometimes the head oriented to the East; the hands crossed; or the face turned up toward heaven. Second, preparations included, the important task of grieving and making peace with relatives, companions and helpers. Grief flowed in both directions. Those about to be bereaved needed to express their grief over imminent loss, and the dying man needed to grieve over the loss of his world. Such mourning was short-lived, but it was not to be denied or obscured. Some measure of suffering was an acceptable part of human dying. The further work of preparation included the reconciliation of the dying man or woman with companions or friends. Finally, the dying person uttered prayers of confession followed by the priest's prayers of absolution.

Where did all this work of preparation take place? Usually, it occurred in the bedchamber of the dying. We must remember, moreover, that the bedroom did not serve on this occasion as a private room. The dying man's bedchamber became a public place to be entered freely by relatives, friends, servants and children. Only 18th century concerns for hygiene led doctors to isolate the dying person in his bedroom. Thenceforward, dying became a private act.

Until the last two hundred years, dying occurred as a public ceremony, but who organized this ceremony? As Aries points out: "The dying person himself served as the master of ceremonies."

How did he learn to do it? Very simply. As a child he had seen others accept responsibility for their own dying. No one excluded him from the patient's room. He knew the protocol. He would do it when his own time came. "Thus, death was familiar and near, evoking no great awe or fear." So, Aries characterizes this whole period as living and dying with a sense of "tamed death."

The contrast today is striking. Instead of dying at home in one's own bedchamber, 80% of Americans die in a hospital or in a nursing home. Earlier, people died in a kind of public ceremony witnessed by a company, including relatives, helpers, friends and children. But today, death often arrives, even for those who have families, secretly in the hospital, unseen except at a technical level by the all-monitoring eye of cardiac equipment. If the patient met death heroically, only the machine would know it.

This absence of human witness alters profoundly the event and one's anticipation of the event. In ancient Greece, heroism required two people: the warrior to perform the heroic deed and the poet to celebrate it. The poet Homer saw death quite literally as the "moment of truth." The Greek word for truth, *Alietheia*, literally means "uncovering." How one dies uncovers or reveals what one is made of. In dying well, the warrior steps out, uncovered, revealed for what he is, courageous rather than cowardly. But the cultural appropriation of this event also requires the poet to celebrate it, to let it stand forth, uncovered, revealed. Thus in failing to acknowledge and honor the dying, the modern community covers over the full truth of death which includes the possibility of human courage before it.

Iin earlier centuries, the person dying organized the event with some sense of protocol. Today, however, others manage dying. We call it management of the terminally ill. A new specialist has been added to interpret and handle the event, the thanatologist, the specialist in death. Still another specialist looms on the horizon, the dolorist, the specialist in grief. In general, however, machines take charge; relatives and friends must make room for them; hospital attendants serve them. Death has become a mechanical process. The person has been robbed of his own dying. The ignorance in which he is often kept deprives him of what earlier cultures felt to be important to a good death-- the forewarning that invited him not simply to participate in medical decisions, but to prepare and to take over his own dying.

Please understand: I do not wish to argue that we should smash the machines or dismantle our huge hi-tech hospitals. I want only to draw attention to the human price we pay with our current practices.

Some Practical Implications for Our Words

One's concept of a good death has bearing on the words and deeds of care-givers. If a good death requires preparation and if preparation ordinarily requires some warning, then we may need to rethink what we say to the dying. Evasion or lying may not offer the best strategy for coping with the crisis. This line of reasoning poses the question of truth-telling in medicine.

Philosophers in the West usually debate the issue of *whether* to tell the truth by appealing either to the consequences of action or to a notion of categorical duty.

The consequentialist believes that the decision whether to tell the truth, to lie, or to withhold the truth depends upon the consequences or results which the decision produces. This philosophical position enjoys support from that cardinal imperative of the ancient

Hippocratic Oath: "do no harm." The imperative to do no harm does not always argue for withholding the truth. Sometimes, to be sure, telling the truth can crush the patient. But, at other times, lying or evading can also cruelly isolate the patient and subject him to a kind of premature burial. Consequentialist reasoning can end up on either side of a decision, though, generally, those who decide not to tell the truth appeal largely to its destructive consequences.

Other moralists ignore the calculation of consequences. They argue categorically, irrespective of consequences, that one ought always to tell the truth. Following the philosopher Immanuel Kant, they argue that we must distinguish between *wrongs* and *harms* in the moral life. Consequentialists take seriously only harms, but the moral life must consider what is *right* and *wrong*, irrespective of the goods and harms that result from action. Lying is always wrong. When I *lie* to another person-- even for his benefit-- I *wrong* him. In lying, I reduce him from a subject to an object, from an end to a means, and therefore I diminish him. I fail to respect him as a rational, self-determining creature. (The U.S. legal system, by the way, deals only with harmful consequences. The plaintiff must prove that the defendant has damaged him by lying, otherwise, he will lose the case. But in moral life, Kantians argue, one may wrong a person by lying even when they do not damage him.)

Another group of philosophers adopts a compromise between two positions, while defending a basic commitment to truth-telling. These moralists distinguish between an *absolute* and a *prima facie* obligation. Truth-telling is not an absolute or categorical obligation because one can imagine circumstances in which telling the truth would so destroy the patient that one needs to withhold it. Nevertheless, truth-telling has a *prima facie* force so powerful that the burden of proof rests on the care-giver to show why, in a particular case, he cannot tell the truth. (I leave out of the discussion of those who lie or tell the truth simply to serve their own self-interest: to protect themselves against a lawsuit, to avoid spending more time with a patient, to keep everything smooth and pleasant for themselves.)

So goes the debate amongst the philosophers and the theologians. In my judgment, however, we need to move beyond the conventional treatment of truth-telling by the philosophers and theologians and ask ourselves the question: what is the whole truth? Do we fully serve the truth merely by dispensing truthful sentences to patients, as though these sentences resembled the pills doctors dispense? Or does the truth include more?

The philosopher, J. L. Austin once drew a distinction, now famous, between two different kinds of sentences: *descriptive* and *performative*. In ordinary descriptive sentences, one describes a given item in the world. (It is raining. The tumor is malignant. The crisis is past.)

In a performative utterance, one does not merely describe the world; one alters the world by introducing an ingredient that would not be there apart from the utterance. Promises-- such as marriage vows and treaties between nations-- are performative utterances. We can call promises performative because they change the world for the parties that enter into them. Treaties affect changes between the nations that agree to them. A wedding ceremony alters the world for two people. (I, John, take thee, Mary, to be my wedded wife. I, Mary, take thee, John, to be my wedded husband.) The wedding ceremony is not a descriptive or even an expressive occasion. John is not obliged to sing an aria with 76 trumpets in the background, telling Mary how much he loves her. Wedding vows are usually very lean and spare. They go to the heart of the occasion very fast, as John and Mary exchange promises and thereby alter one another's world. And, of course, because a marriage is world-altering, divorce, even under the best circumstances, is a difficult and painful event.

A tacit promise, therefore, marks the professional relationship of the doctor to his or her patient, or the lawyer to the client. (Tell me about your worries and your physical complaints. I promise to take care of you.) That tacit promise begins to alter the world of the worried and stricken patient. Correspondingly, to break the promise can add to the patient's misery. Thus, the terms and circumstances under which a professional can withdraw from a case becomes an important matter in professional ethics.

Clearly, the dilemma of truth-telling in Western medicine has chiefly turned on the issue of descriptive speech. Should the doctor tell the patient he has a malignancy, or not? If not, may he lie or must he merely withhold the truth? The distinction, however, between descriptive and performative speech expands the question of the truth in professional life. The talented lawyer, in an important way, alters the world of his troubled client when he tells him that he will take his case. The doctor not only tells descriptive truths, he also makes or implies promises. (I will see you next Tuesday-- or-- despite the fact that I cannot cure you, I will not abandon you; I will care for you.) Morally, the professional must face the question not simply of telling truths, but of *being true* to his or her promises. Conversely, the patient's total situation includes not only the disease that afflicts him, but also whether others abandon him or stand by him in extremity. The fidelity of the professional will not eliminate the disease or the crime but it can affect mightily the context in which the trouble runs its course. What the professional has to offer the client is not only diagnostic accuracy and efficiency in treatment but also fidelity.

Such fidelity begins, then, to affect the resolution of the dilemma of truth-telling itself. Perhaps more patients could accept the descriptive truth if they experienced the performative truth. Perhaps also they would be more inclined to believe in the doctor's performative utterances if they were not handed utterly false diagnoses or false promises. That is why a cautiously wise medieval physician once advised his colleagues: "Promise only fidelity!"

Most philosophers wrestle only with the quandary of *whether* to tell the truth; they do not attend sufficiently to the further question as to *how* one tells it. Physicians know, however, that the question is not simply *what* you say, but also how you say it, when you say it, and who says it. Such questions of correct procedure, form, style, and timing also bear importantly on professional ethics.

Personal style requires more than an attractive packaging of what one has to say. Style springs from a deeper metaphysical and psychological perception, a sense for what the Stoics call "the fitting," a discretion and discernment that goes deeper than mere tact, a feel for what is congruent with reality. Without such discretion, the professional does not perceive or respond to the whole truth. He may tell the truth, but he does not truly serve the truth when he tells it. He may be using the truth to serve his own vanity, or to satisfy his craving for power, or to indulge himself in the role of nag, policeman, judge, or even torturer of his or her patient.

The question, "how," immediately poses the question of the types of language with which we communicate with one another. Americans, I believe, rely on at least four possible resources in language: first, direct, blunt speech; second, circumlocution and double-talk, third, silence; and fourth, what I would call indirect discourse.

First, Americans rely chiefly on direct, blunt talk. Sometimes, of course, forceful, direct speech entirely fits the patient's needs. But I would not want to argue that all patients should hear the truth in pitiless detail. Certainly, there are cases in which the patient would fall apart under the weight of it.

Second, we rely on language of circumlocution and double-talk. Professionals especially are masters at double-talk. Their education supplies them with a technical vocabulary that allows them to state the truth so technically that while they pride themselves in their scientific scrupulosity, the truth, in fact, passes through the patient like a dose of salts-- received but not absorbed.

Third, we sometimes rely on silence as a way of sharing. A courtship enters a new stage when a young couple does not feel obliged to chatter nervously, when the young man and woman are sufficiently at home with one another to share silently. But silence can also lapse into an incommunicative withdrawal or avoidance. Or, even worse, in family life, silence can serve as a form of punishment. The mother or father finds what the child has done so unspeakable that the child feels excommunicated and condemned beyond appeal before his utterly silent parent.

Fourth, we rely on the language of indirection, in such serious matters as religion, love, and death. I do not need to emphasize the importance of indirection in religion to a people familiar with the Koan. One illustration will suffice from the West. The pious Jew does not speak directly the innermost name of God-- Jahweh-- but refers to God indirectly through such names as Adonoi. The people of Israel never see God directly. They deal indirectly with God through the prophet Moses who, in turn, never sees God face-to-face.

The same protocol of indirection guides us in the delicacies of courtship. A young man invites a young woman out for dinner. After dinner, he mentions that he has just purchased some recordings of Mozart's music and he asks her whether she would like to come up to his apartment to listen to Mozart-- mostly. And she replies, "Thank you very much, but I really don't care for Mozart, Goodnight!"

My illustration is not very good. The exchange of words between two young people is too transparent. In a variety of more subtle ways, young people talk about one thing while meaning another. Thus, sparing themselves the awkwardness of too blunt a proposal and too blunt a rejection.

The language of indirection can be important in medical crises. I hope you do not object to a personal example. When my father was in his mid-sixties and already suffered from cancer of the pharynx, he experienced severe pains in his legs. I took him to see a new doctor since his own doctor had just died of a heart attack. Tests showed that cancer had metastasized into his liver and elsewhere, and he had only six months to live. The physician informed me of his condition, leaving me to speak with my father. I wondered what I would say upon seeing him. But before I could say anything, my father, who was a man of few words, said, Go easy, Bill."

Those compressed words said little directly, but, indirectly, they said a lot. In saying, Go easy, Bill," I believe that my father was not avoiding the fact of his death. He was saying, rather, that he knew that he was dying, but at the same time, he was signalling to his eldest son, "Spare me, my son, one of your seminar-length discussions of the subject, please." For at the same time that he let me know that he was dying, he was signalling to me the distance that he wanted to maintain between himself and the event and himself and me. Eventually, it fell upon my only sister, the fourth child in the family, the beloved daughter, to speak more directly, more gently, to my father than I could have managed to speak.

So we depend upon the virtue of wisdom, prudence or discernment to solve problems in truth-telling beyond the clumsy reach of a book of rules.

Some Practical Implications for Our Deeds

Our concept of a good death also has bearing on our deeds as caregivers. I will concentrate particularly on the question of hospital policies toward the dying. But I should concede at the outset that such policies do not address the problem of death at its deepest level.

The poet T. S. Eliot once said that we face two types of problems in life for which two different questions are appropriate. The first problem poses the question, "What are we going to do about it?" That question asks for a relatively pragmatic, technical, programmatic solution to a problem. In this case, it asks for the development of good hospital policies. But a second type of problem poses for us a deeper question, "How does one behave towards it?" This second question demands from us more than a technical solution to a problem; it challenges our own self-definition as we struggle to find a fitting and decorous way to respond to an awesome event.

Most of the deeper moral challenges in life are of the latter kind: the intricacies of courtship between two people; the conflicts between the generations (adolescence is hardly a problem that parents solve; they struggle at best to learn how to live with the turbulence of their adolescent child), the mystery of fading powers, and death. All these deeper challenges in life confront us not simply with something to do, but with someone to be.

The eighty year old widow of a university president once said to me, "When my husband died, I realized that there was nothing I could do about his death. The only question I faced was whether I could rise to the occasion."

The great film maker Kurasawa also dealt with this deeper challenge in his film, "Ikiru," the account of the elderly, unimaginative, dried out, routinized, stingy, civil servant, who, when he discovered that he had stomach cancer, began to break out of the narrow confines of his former life and came alive, for the first time, as a human being.

Kurasawa showed in that film that Eliot's two levels of problems overlap. Death confronts the old man both with something to do but also with someone to be.

Conceding this distinction, we now turn to the more superficial, pragmatic, yet important problems that professionals face in developing appropriate hospital policies for care of the dying. Debates on these issues in the United States usually polarize between two absolutistic positions: the pro-lifers and the pro-quality-of-lifers.

The pro-lifers see life as the absolute good and, correspondingly, death as the absolute evil. Therefore, they define the physician as an unconditional fighter against death. Were the physician ever to "pull out the plug" on the dying patient, he would be pulling out the plug on his own identity.

The pro-quality-of-lifers see wealth or abundance of life as the absolute good. Correspondingly, they see suffering as the absolute evil. Therefore, they would support policies favoring the possibility of active euthanasia to relieve the patient of his suffering.

I would urge a more moderate view than either of these two absolutistic positions. In my judgement, we do not understand the moral life aright when we see it as a grim struggle of life against death or quality-of-life against poverty. Neither should our political life disintegrate into fierce conflict of pro-lifers against quality-of-lifers, each heaping epithets on the other, each charging the other with moral blindness. Both absolutistic positions are ultimately too shrill to control their advocates' own excesses: one group clamors in panic for life at all cost; the other proclaims, "Give me quality-of-life or give me death." A more moderate philosophical and religious perspective suggests that decisions should vary in different cases: sometimes to relieve suffering, at other times to resist death. But in any event, decisions should not spring from that fear and despair which often creates the absolutist in ethics.

I will not try to develop here the philosophical and religious reasons for this perspective. Suffice it to say that this more moderate position has two general consequences for the medical profession and its use of technology. First, the profession should not define itself wholly by a fight against death. When determined exclusively by that fight, the profession presses for prolongation of life at any cost. Physicians should be free to respond to patients' requests to cease and desist in the effort to prolong life when treatment can no longer serve the health of the host. A physician does not always have the duty to fight pneumonia if such death has become acceptable to the patient, in preference to death by extraordinarily painful, irreversible and protracted cancer. There is, after all, a time to live and a time to die. There is a right to die.

At the same time, however, neither physicians nor the society at large ought to prize so highly life's quality that they solve the problem of suffering by eliminating the sufferer. This solution to the problem of evil, propounded by the advocates of active euthanasia, denies the patient's capacity to cope with life once terminal pain and suffering have appeared. It assumes that life has peaked somewhere on a hill behind the ill person and that all else ahead slopes downward toward oblivion. They doubt that end-time itself can be suffused with the human.

With this much in hand, we turn now to distinctions important in health care and hospital policies, the distinctions between: 1) maximal treatment and optimal care; 2) starting and stopping machines; 3) ordinary and extraordinary means, and 4) allowing someone to die and mercy killing.

1) Maximal treatment and optimal care.

An unconditional war against death wrongly assumes that maximal treatment is always optimal care. However, maximal medical assault by invasive diagnostic procedures, by aggressive and complicated drug management, by enthusiastic cutting and burning, does not automatically provide optimal care for patients. Often such treatment merely distracts from the use of precious time for what really matters. At the worst, such treatment can produce a patient who resembles that

Vietnam village which American planes destroyed by bombs in the course of liberating it.   Fortunately, therefore, some teaching hospitals-- precisely those institutions which by virtue of resources are most tempted to wage all-out war-- have pulled back from total war against death.

The Massachusetts General Hospital (MGH) in the USA has adopted procedures recommended by its Critical Care Committee that would classify critically ill patients into four groups and establish different levels of treatment in each group.

Class A: Maximal therapeutic effort without reservation.

Class B: Maximal therapeutic effort without reservation but with daily evaluation.

Class C: Selective limitation of therapeutic measures patient is not an appropriate candidate for admission to an Intensive Care Unit. . .

Class D: All therapy can be discontinued though maximum comfort to the patient may be continued or instituted   (Massachusetts General Hospital Report)

The Massachusetts General Hospital (MGH) Report, by implication at least, dissolves two distinctions that previously established for some physicians' and moralists' clear-cut limits on therapeutic efforts-- the distinctions between starting and stopping machines and between ordinary and heroic measures. In my judgement, the report correctly abandons both distinctions for the more apt criterion of the patient's welfare.

2) Starting and stopping the machines.

Physicians commonly feel that they have discretion in a case only before they start the machines. Once the machines start, they lose the option of letting the patient die.   This position makes sense psychologically. To pull the plug, once vital signs have been restored, seems too much like killing.   The distinction, however, between starting and stopping the machines misleads at two points. First, it might encourage a physician to fail to turn on the machines, for fear of producing a monstrosity, when he should turn them on, and have the benefit of a more informed choice. He can subsequently turn them off should the machine prove useless in serving the patient's health. Second, the distinction converts a machine from an instrument into a fatality. It assumes that once the machines are running, they move beyond the reach of human decision-making. The machines are no longer anyone's responsibility. This submissive attitude toward the equipment repeats the more general submissiveness that the patient (if competent) and his family already feel toward the hospital as an institution. Once within the precincts of the hospital, the patient often feels that he must comply with its routines and decisions. The hospital, its staff, and its equipment confront him as fate. He feels like the young visitor at the whorehouse who believes that he has freedom only before he enters its doors. Once past the front door he must submit to what goes on there. He is in the hands of professionals.

The MGH Report rightly subordinates the operation of the machines to the patient's welfare since it allows for the reclassification of patients and provides for daily evaluation of patients in Class B. The report also establishes procedures for such acts as turning off mechanical ventilators at that point in therapy when the machine may offer maximal treatment but no longer optimal care.

3) Rejecting the distinction between heroic and ordinary measures.

Similarly, the MGH Report rejects the medical distinction between ordinary and heroic measures. This distinction traditionally lets physicians withdraw therapy only if the therapy could be characterized as heroic. While I am sympathetic to the final intent of the distinction insofar as it allows some patients to die, the distinction makes too much of the status of the means. In some cases, it can be said conscientiously that the withdrawal of heroic measures best serves the patient's well-being, but so also the withdrawal of something as ordinary today as penicillin may just as aptly serve his welfare.

The MGH Report, in effect, relaxes the distinction between ordinary and heroic when it provides for classification D, under which all therapy (but not all efforts to provide comfort) can be discontinued. The crucial distinction does not fall between ordinary and heroic measures, but between two conditions of patients with two different sets of needs: those for whom efforts to cure are appropriate and those for whom efforts at remedy are in vain but for whom care remains imperative. A given procedure, whether ordinary or heroic, should be evaluated as to whether it offers optimal care. Otherwise, the physician may, in fact, neglect the patient by gagging him with the irrelevant and by denying to him what he truly needs. As Paul

Ramsey writes in his *Patient As Person*, "Just as it would be negligence to the sick to treat them as if they were about to die, so it is another sort of 'negligence' to treat the dying as if they are going to get well or might get well" (Ramsey, 1970.). The MGH Report, with its provision for daily evaluations, attempts to eliminate the negligence of misplaced treatment.

4) Mercy killing vs. allowing to die.

Finally, some moralists would argue that the distinction between allowing to die and mercy killing is hypocritical, quibbling over technique. They call allowing to die "passive euthanasia" and mercy killing "active euthanasia" and collapse the distinction between the two.   Since the patient dies-- whether by acts of omission or commission-- what matters the route the patient took there? By either procedure he ends up dead.   Since modern procedures, moreover, have made dying at the hands of the experts and their machines such a prolonged and painful business, pressure has built up behind the active euthanasia movement which asserts not simply the right to die but the right to be killed.

Other moralists believe that the distinction between allowing to die and mercy killing is worth preserving. They would favor provision for allowing to die but oppose killing for mercy.   The euthanasia movement, these critics believe, basically engineers death rather than faces dying.   Euthanasia would bypass dying to get one dead as quickly as possible. It proposes to relieve suffering by knocking out the interval between the two states, living and dead. The emotional impulse behind the euthanasia movement is understandable in an age when dying has become such an inhumanly endless business.   The movement opposes the horrors of a purely technical death by using technique to eliminate the victim. But it fails to appreciate our human capacity to rise to the occasion of our death.

The alternative I have outlined argues, at least in principle, that warning can provoke good; that with forewarning and time for preparation, reconciliation can take place; and that advanced grieving by those about to be bereaved may ease their pain. Some psychiatrists have observed that those bereaved who lose someone accidentally have a more difficult time recovering from the loss than those who have suffered through a period of illness before the death. Those who have lost a close relative by accident are more likely to experience what Geoffrey Gorer has called "limitless grief." The community, moreover, needs its aged and dependent, its sick and its dying, and the virtues which they sometimes evince-- the virtues of humility, courage, and patience-- just as much as the community needs the virtues of justice and love manifest in the agents of its care. Thus, on the whole, I am in favor of a social policy that would take seriously the notion of allowing to die, rather than killing for mercy; that is, which would recognize that moment in illness when it is no longer meaningful to bend every effort to cure or to prolong life, when it is fitting to allow patients to do their own dying. This policy seems most consonant with the obligations of the community to care and the patient to finish his course.

I can, to be sure, imagine rare circumstances in which I hope I would have the courage to kill for mercy-- when the patient is utterly beyond human care, terminal, and in excruciating pain. A neurosurgeon once showed a group of us the picture of a Vietnam casualty who had lost all four limbs in a land of mine explosion. The catastrophe had reduced him to a trunk with his face transfixed in horror. On the battlefield, I would hope that I would have the courage to kill the sufferer with mercy. But hard cases do not always make good laws or wise social policies. Regularized mercy killings would too quickly relieve the community of its obligation to provide good care.

Further, we should not always expect the law to provide us with full protection and coverage for what, in rare circumstances, we may need morally to do. Sometimes, the moral life calls us out into a no-man's land where we cannot expect total security and protection under the law. But whoever said that the moral life was easy?

References

Aries, Phillipe (1974). *Western Attitudes Towards Death*, Baltimore, Maryland: Johns Hopkins Press.

Massachusetts General Hospital Report (1976). Optimum care for hopelessly ill patients; a report of the Clinical Care Committee of the Massachusetts General Hospital. *The New England Journal of Medicine*, Volume 295:7 pp. 362-64.

Ramsey, Paul (1970). *The Patient As a Person*. New Haven, Connecticut: Yale University Press.

Euthanasia and Care for the Dying in the Orthodox Tradition

Vigen Guroian

"Whether, therefore, we live or die we belong to the Lord."

Romans 14: 8

In July of 1991 the *Washington Post* ran a two-part front-page feature on the history of Baby Rena and her tragic death at the age of 18 months from complications of AIDS and heart disease. The first article of the series opened in this fashion:

> Murray Polack, a physician at Children's Hospital, felt the time had come to change the rules. His eighteen-month old patient, Baby Rena, was dying, a victim of AIDS and heart disease. For six weeks, ever since her arrival at the intensive-care unit in late January, she had been breathing only with the help of a respirator. She was in so much pain that Polack kept her constantly sedated. When nurses performed even the simplest procedure, such as weighing her, her blood pressure shot up and tears streamed down her face. But a tube in her throat made it impossible for her to utter a sound (Weiser, July 14, 1991).

Pollack had been called in to take over the case after Baby Rena was brought to the hospital on January 30th for what became her final stay. She died at Children's Hospital on March 25th. From the outset,

Pollack judged Baby Rena's case probably "futile." Keeping her on the respirator was not a life-saving measure so much as it was an intrusion into her dying process which only intensified and prolonged her suffering. Pollack argued that he and the medical staff had "a responsibility to do what's best for Rena . . . and to give her the appropriate care-- and that is not always giving her all care" (Weiser, July 15, 1991).

Pollack was not advocating mercy killing, rather, he wanted those responsible for her care to "let go"-- to let Rena die the death she was dying as well as possible. This he judged meant removing her from intensive care and the respirator. Sedation was indicated to relieve her severe pain; and death would likely follow sooner rather than later.

Children's Hospital required consent of parents or legal guardians before a patient could be removed from a respirator, but Rena's mother had abandoned her at birth and Rena was the ward of the District government. The hospital then sought permission from the government to take her off the respirator, but the government denied the request. Her foster parents had no legal standing in the decision. Nevertheless, their objections to Pollack's recommendations were strong and eventually heard. The parents believed that God had told them to "take the child, and rear her in the nurture and admonition of God's word . . . and to battle the spirits of infirmity" (Weiser, July 14, 1991). They demanded that her treatment "be motivated by a spiritual sense of obedience to God" (Weiser, July 15, 1991).

In the Baby Rena case, the foster parents, the pastor of their church, and their friends were important actors. They all professed a Christian belief in the sanctity of life and God's lordship over living and dying, yet by all the standards of the Orthodox Christian tradition, I cannot find good cause to agree with either their reasoning or their judgement. There are resources and reasons in the Christian tradition to draw a distinction between direct killing in health care settings and allowing to die. The former is rightly to be called euthanasia and is morally wrong. The latter is not euthanasia and may sometimes be what Christian conscience requires-- it does not fall under moral prohibition.

Baby Rena's foster parents' appeals to God and His law only served to blur this important distinction between direct killing and letting die. Due to their overly simplified definition of God's sovereignty over life, and their hard identification of sickness and death with demonic spirits, the foster parents of Baby Rena equated good care for the dying with absolute and unlimited care. But biblical and Christian ethics are more nuanced than this. Christians are permitted sometimes to let life ebb away in its natural course, while continuing care to relieve pain and provide comfort to the dying person. Yet how is it that Baby Rena's foster parents, who were religious people, could not entertain this possibility?

Many persons in our society who profess to be Christians discount such calibrated care for the dying as against God's will. This religious vitalism which mystifies human existence is not consistent with Orthodox Christian faith. What we observe in the foster parents' kind of religion is a dualism which separates physical existence from spiritual existence. This mistaken and misguided form of faith is what moved an otherwise loving father to insist that the extreme physical pain which his small child was enduring be permitted to go on. For the sake of her spiritual existence, he would not allow his daughter's dying to follow its course. We are then bound to this question: "What does it mean to care for the spiritual well-being of a loved one who is dying if that care does not regard the physical pain and dying which she is enduring?"

Baby Rena's foster father was quoted repeatedly as saying that it was necessary to be sure of what God wanted. Yet was this not already obvious at the level of Baby Rena's suffering and dying flesh? What could the parents possibly have been waiting for to reveal God's will? The judgement of imminent death and the futility of medical treatment is a medical question. God does not need respirators to work miracles, but God entrusts determinations of whether we are biologically dying to our physicians, whether they themselves trust in Him or not. Baby Rena's foster parents were further from knowing God's will or from knowing where to find it than they could ever have imagined.

In the *Washington Post* articles, Dr. Pollack was quoted as having said, "We have a responsibility to do what's best for Rena . . . and to give her the appropriate care-- and that is not always giving her *all* [italics mine] care. This was the crucial issue in Baby Rena's case." There is no indication in either article that Dr. Pollack was a believing Jew or Christian. Nevertheless, his judgement, I maintain, was more consistent than the foster parents' with the conclusion to which a conscientious Christian trying to do the right thing in that circumstance should have drawn. A mature faith in the God of Jewish and Christian scriptures includes the assurance that even our dying cannot pass beyond God's love and care. This confidence has provided persons of science and faith with the wisdom and the courage to apply limits to life-saving interventions in medical practice while also enabling them to hold to absolute limits upon the taking of the lives of terminally ill persons.

Why Euthanasia is Wrong

There are important Christian reasons which weigh against euthanasia. I am here accepting the definition which today is commonly given to euthanasia. Euthanasia in its word origins means simply, "a good death." However, in our time it has come to mean choosing death as a remedy or end for people suffering from debilitating or terminal illness. The deliberate putting to death of helpless or infirm persons cannot be countenanced from within the Christian faith. Nor are the commonly invoked formal distinctions between voluntary, involuntary, or nonvoluntary euthanasia very helpful. The end sought is the same. Let us make no mistake about it. Euthanasia is the taking of life, whatever the intentions might be of those who help people to die.

While we must reject euthanasia, the contemporary debate over it does open opportunities for serious discussion about pastoral care for the sick and dying. Euthanasia raises difficult issues about when treatment should be terminated and suffering be attended to in order to help those who are dying die as painless as possible. This society's drift into what the late Southern Catholic writer Walker Percy called the "thanatos syndrome" requires Orthodox Christians to be especially clear about how they regard death theologically in their efforts to speak in ethical terms about care for the dying. There are enormous resources, especially in the Orthodox rites of holy unction and burial, for doing the morally correct thing for persons who are sick and dying people. I will devote the balance of my remarks to an exploration of these resources.

The Byzantine Rite of Holy Unction: On Sin and Death

"It falsifies the Christian message," wrote the Russian Orthodox theologian Fr. Alexander Schmemann, "to present and to preach Christianity as essentially life-affirming-- without referring this affirmation to the death of Christ and therefore to the very fact of death; to pass over in silence the fact that for Christianity, death is

not only the end, but indeed is the very reality of *this world*"
(Schmemann, 1973). Fr. Schmemann penned these words while
arguing that Christians are in jeopardy of abandoning their Christ-
centered realism about death. They, like many others in this society,
are becoming persuaded that it is their job to "justify' death as natural
and help people to accept death as if there is nothing horrible about it.
But, as Alexander Schmemann insists, "Christianity is not
reconciliation with death, it is the revelation of death, and it reveals
death because it is the revelation of Life." Death is the enemy of Life.
It is something to be faced in its awful reality and "to be destroyed,
not a mystery to be explained" (Schmemann, 1973). Christ wept at
the grave of Lazarus. He did not offer a sermon on the meaning of
death or rhapsodize about how wonderful a fellow Lazarus was in life
and how much joy he brought into all our lives. Instead, he raised
Lazarus from death. At no time in his ministry when visiting with the
sick and dying did Jesus try to persuade his listeners that death is
something natural or beautiful. Instead, he did what he could to cure
the sick. Yet only by voluntarily giving up his own life and dying a
death like ours was Jesus able to exhaust and defeat the power of
death. Only in our dying and being resurrected with Christ is our
sickness unto death cured.

Nowhere in Orthodox Christian practice is this conviction about
death and how it has been overcome more central and more
powerfully expressed than in the rites of holy unction and burial.
These rites present us with another belief which is of first importance
to a Christian approach to care for the dying. It is the biblical
persuasion that death and sickness cannot be understood apart from
sin, that "death is the wages of sin," (Romans 6:23) and "the sting of
death is sin" (Corinthians 15:56). The common misunderstanding that
the anointing of the sick is just about curing physical or psychological
illness testifies to how forgetful we have become of the biblical
correlation of sin and death. Anointing of the sick and dying is, in
fact, primarily about penance and forgiveness of sins. The deeper
meaning of healing in the rites of holy unction is lost if the
connections between sin and death and repentance and forgiveness are
forgotten. The Byzantine rite of holy unction thus opens with Psalms
143 and 51.

> Have mercy on me, O God,
>   according to your steadfast love;

according to your abundant mercy
   blot out my transgressions.
Wash me thoroughly from my
   iniquity,
   and cleanse me from my sin.

For I know my transgressions,
   and my sin is ever before me.
Against you, you alone, have I sinned
   and done what is evil in your sight,
   so that you are justified in you sentence . . .
Indeed, I was born guilty,
   a sinner when my mother conceived me . . .

Create in me a clean heart,
O God, and put a new and right spirit
   within me . . .
Restore to me the joy of your
   salvation, and sustain in me a willing
   spirit.

Psalm 51: 1-10, 12

In the Old Testament, the Hebrew for salvation comes from *yasha,* meaning "to be at large," to save from a danger. Salvation is closely connected with the notion of the healing of body and soul. God delivers us-- literally snatches us-- not only from our personal enemies and from persecution and the like, but from sickness and from the power of death. In the New Testament, the Greek *sozo* is derived from *saos,* which means "healthy." Prayer and penance for the sin which attaches to all "flesh" and makes that flesh subject to a corruptible death (the destruction of the unity of body and soul) issue form the belief that God wants to heal all of our infirmities. Furthermore, we are given assurance by Christ's words and deeds that this healing belongs to the whole process of salvation. Jesus bore *mortal* flesh to gain for us a foretaste of victory over sin and death where those twin enemies had taken up apparently secure citadel. The healing done by Jesus is not merely a metaphor or external sign for salvation. It is a deep symbol and sacrament of salvation binding together heaven and earth, leading to eternal life. All of Jesus' miraculous healings foreshadow His victorious death on the cross through which we are given entrance into the eternal kingdom of His Father.

God, whose love is steadfast and whose mercy is abundant, could never euthanize. In Jesus' life, death and resurrection we learn that God intends to save us for eternal life. From a Christian standpoint, the euthanists' motives, however "humanitarian" or well-intended, cannot justify what they do. The aim of their euthanizing counts more than their motives in an evaluation of the rightness or wrongness of the act. That aim is contrary to everything God intends for us and does for us. There is a difference between a God-centered humanism and man-centered humanitarianisms. Christians must insist upon the difference. While they might grant the good intent of those who, in the name of humanitarianisms, practice euthanasia, Christians must condemn euthanization as wrong and sinful.

The Images of Life and Death in the Armenian Rite of Burial for the Layman

Anointing of the sick and dying is no substitute for medical care and treatment. Anointing is not a kind of Christian magic. Penance and asking God to forgive the sick person's personal sins, however, are healing practices which hold an understanding of health, broader and deeper than the narrow naturalistic and mechanistic meanings health often carries in modern medical practice.

I want to turn next to the Armenian Rite for the Burial of a Layman. It continues the subjects of penance and atonement contained in the Byzantine rite of holy unction. It sets forth, however, a far more exhaustive theology of death. The centerpiece of that theology is the belief that God became like us in order to cure us of death. The rite provides a strong basis in Christian belief that care for the dying is compassionate care for that flesh among us which is near to the end of the perishing in which we all participate from birth through death. We must value this flesh not only because God created it but because the Son of God made it his own form of living and dying. Despair over the perishing of flesh represented in acts of suicide and euthanasia, therefore, are not only unreasonable but irreverent.

The great prayer attributed to St. Basil in the Armenian rite for the burial of a layman sets forth in vivid images the principal theological tenets upon which this ethic is founded.

We thank thee, Father of our Lord Jesus Christ who because of thy love of mankind has visited us, and saved [us] from the machinations of the traducer [of] the race of men that were driven out and banished afar.

For Satan was jealous of us, and drove us out of eternal life by his deceits and wiles, proscribing and banishing us unto our destruction and ruin. But thou, O God, who art benevolent and lovest man, didst not permit the bitterness of his poisoned fangs to remain in us. Wherefore thou didst summon death, and poured it out upon creatures, in order that the wickedness that had befallen might not remain immortal: but by removing us from this life, and cutting us from our sins, the punishment of the beneficent One became salvation.

But in the last of days thou didst send thy only- begotten Son beloved in the image of the death of sin; and he condemned sin in his own body, and by his voluntary crucifixion shattered the hosts of the enemy. He became the firstfruits of them that slept, and by his divinely marvellous resurrection he invited us to share in his own immortality.

Now this thy servant believing in him has been baptized into the death of thy Christ . . . Remit to this man his debts incurred either willingly or unwillingly, and heal all the wounds which the disincarnate enemy hath inflicted . . . .

And now do thou heal his wounds, and convey him peacefully past the principalities of darkness . . . and efface the handwriting of their influences and inworkings, which they have sown in him and vouchsafe to him a goodly journey . . . [L]et him through [the path of the Tree of Life so that he may] arrive at the place of safety where all thy saints are massed and wait for the great wedding, when the great God and Savior shall appear, Jesus Christ, at the sound of the great trumpet . . . Then . . . at the glance of the judge the earth shall be shaken, and the sealed sepulchres be opened. The bodies that were turned to dust are built up afresh, and the spirits swooping down like eagles reach them and array themselves in the incorruptible body.

In this prayer, virtually all of the church's theology of death appears. Yet within a culture where fewer and fewer people believe in a soul or the immortality of flesh and spirit, those that pray this prayer and take it to heart as physicians, nurses, or family members in their care for the dying are bound to look odd to even the most good-willed observer. What is perhaps most incomprehensible to modern people is the belief that death's reality is more than biological or physical. This prayer and the whole of the Christian tradition inform us that death is also spiritual. Our dying extends beyond the otherwise medically useful fiction of a precise moment of death measured in terms of the cessation in function of the brain or the "closing down" of the body's system of vital organs. Paradoxically, spiritual death is something which can happen to people in life while they might be freed from the same lying in the grave. Spiritual death, in the classical Christian understanding, is defined in strict relation to the body. The Armenian rite portrays this death as expulsion from the garden with the Tree of Life. This means separation from God who is the sole Giver of life. Spiritual death is not the opposite of immortality. Only God has the power to annihilate our existence, and God will not will it. But we have the power to reject that true Life "which was the light of man" (John 1:2). Sin is the character of the creature alienated from true Life. This brings a death which is an immortal death-- an unceasing separation from God. Immortal death is not non-existence, but a kind of existence in separation from God. The opposite of this immortal death is life in eternity with God. In the Armenian prayer, the original sin and its eternal consequences is symbolically depicted through the image of a journey back through death to the garden of the Tree of Life where the saints await "the great wedding, when the great God and Savior shall appear, Jesus Christ."

Death understood in its spiritual reality threatens personal existence with one other form of separation or alienation. This is the separation of the soul from the body. This corruptible death is the actual decomposition of the body-soul unity which makes up the living person. It is a kind of fading away of the image of God in the human being. The anthem of St. John of Damascus in the Byzantine rite of burial exclaims, "I weep and wail when I think upon death, and behold our beauty, fashioned after the image of God, lying in the disfigured, dishonored, bereft of form." The Armenian prayer states that such a death "was summon[ed] by God and poured . . . out upon creatures in order that the wickedness that had befallen might not remain immortal." Note that the prayer does not say that God invented death. Rather, God allowed the natural inclination of the creature toward dissolution to go its way.

While this complete dissolution of the person is death in all its horror, the very process of dying itself holds a terror common for all human beings, even those uninformed by such an understanding of personal existence. This terrifying experience anticipates the final control of our body and with it our very identity and our whole world, both personal and impersonal. For it is only in and through this body, this "flesh" in its wholeness and relation with our psychic existence, that we are able to participate in the world. (This capacity and state of being which we are losing we call health). The experience of the dissolution of our being and loss of our world is more profound than any secular psychological or social science is able to comprehend because it reaches beyond the scope of such science, beyond space and temporality into eternity.

But the Easter faith proclaims that even this death has been overcome once and for all in Christ Jesus. Christ came to destroy and abolish corruptible death. The physical death which medicine knows, studies, and tries to delay is not something that Christ necessarily came to abolish. Had Christ abolished this form of death He would have had to abolish this world which was created through Him by His Father; for "physical' death is a part of this world as much as birth and growth are. Instead, Christ has taken the sting, the spiritual poison of sin, out of death by denying it a final triumph over life. Through his own voluntary death on the Cross, Christ has transformed our dying into a passage and entrance into a fuller life of communion and love with God and His saints.

The Church and Caring for the Dying

Thus far, I have identified two aspects of Christian faith itself, which require us to respond compassionately and in non-lethal ways toward the sick and dying. These are hard truths in any time. They certainly run against the utilitarianism, narcissism and therapeutic ethos of our own time. The first is that sin and death are mystically related. This calls for penance, not merely understood in punitive or juridical terms, but as a healing sacrament. The second is the work of healing and hope through the Incarnation and Resurrection. I want to review these as a way of closing.

There are those who are bound to object to the extraordinary attention given to sin and penance in the Byzantine and Armenian rites. They will want to dismiss sin and penance as inappropriate for pastoral care of the sick and dying. What a cruel thing to impose on people who are weakened with sickness or facing their own imminent demise. It is true that penance can be twisted and misused by those who are commissioned to practice the theology of the church in pastoral and medical care settings. Condescension and a punitive desire often turn what is supposed to be healing into another form of torment for the afflicted. There exist among the clergy and laity of every church the contemporary counterparts of Job's so-called friends, who either out of an inflexible orthodoxy or more subjective causes only add to the suffering of the afflicted. They either judge the sick and dying in the place of God or remind them incessantly of their failures.

These misuses of a penitential theology, however, do not discredit the profound and practical wisdom of the church in placing repentance and forgiveness at the center of its prayers for the sick and dying. This practice makes perfect sense in light of the Gospels and indeed the whole of scripture. We have seen already that the Bible and Orthodox tradition hold that sickness is often enmeshed, "consciously or not, in the complexities of sin, personal and/or social." This does not mean that we should think of sickness as a direct punishment for individual sins. Jesus rejected such a view (John 9: 1-3) in the story of the blind man of whom St. John writes in his Gospel. Nevertheless, a connection of sickness and death with personal sin is not ruled out. This biblical truth is confirmed in "the statistical correlation of [voluntary] overeating [gluttony] and smoking with heart disease, or sexual license with venereal disease and AIDS. It is even sometimes pastorally appropriate to remind persons of the sins they have committed and forgotten or repressed when a connection between such behavior and their sickness can be understood.

The Byzantine and Armenian rites wisely encompass the personal burden of guilt and remorse which weighs ever so much more heavily upon persons who are sick or dying. In these circumstances, the sins that one has committed over a lifetime can suddenly return and devastatingly haunt a person. This guilt can confound whatever meaning we have made out of our lives. Thus there is a need for some accounting for our sins. This need for forgiveness and reconciliation is respected in the Armenian rite for Communion of the Sick. The rubrics say that the priest shall take "the saving mystery and the cross and censor . . . and go to the sick man . . . But it is *fitting* [italics mine] that the sick man should first hold converse with his intimate friends or with anyone else with all vigilance and circumspection. And if he has any grudge against anyone, he shall forgive him."

The church's theology of resurrection and eternal life is a source of hope for the sick and dying. But it too, like the theology of sin and penance, can be abused by those who would care for them. A condescending cheerfulness and insistence on Christian hope can be just as alienating and tormenting as an insensitive or morbid preoccupation with sin and making amends. I think the strong emphasis on sin and penance in the Byzantine and Armenian rites helps to prevent this cheapening of the hope in the resurrection. Christ died for the *sins* of all to remove the curse of guilt and abolish death, with its sting of emptiness and desolation. Through his dying and our participation in it, death is transformed into a passage to eternal life. Death, which was the wages of sin, becomes the end of sins. God does not remove all the pain and anguish of dying. Christ himself experienced that pain and anguish. Living in the hope of the resurrection, however, means the faith that God can reach even into the abyss of nonexistence to confer life.

Conclusion

In this essay I have tried to show the theological basis for a Christian understanding of death, euthanasia, and care for the dying. Yet I caution that we cannot assume that our Christian convictions will get much of a hearing presently in this society. We, ourselves, have lost an understanding of these convictions. This compounds the problem. Nevertheless, God would have us put into practice these convictions in our care for the sick and dying. The society in which we live was once deeply informed by biblical faith. This is no longer so. Our whole society is fast losing memory of the reasons why it has objected to the casual taking of life or why we bother to give care to people who are going to die anyway. In view of these trends, I believe that Christians must concentrate more of their energies into the ongoing life of the church and instruction in scripture. The ethic I have described is firstly a church-centered ethic. It is an ethic founded in the cardinal convictions and stories of Christian faith. It is an ethic of people formed by the scriptures and prayer. Naturally, this ethic is located within a larger tradition of pastoral theology and practice. Care for the sick and dying begins with care for the healthy and living. The sacraments, Christian catechesis, and preaching are the precedents and in some real sense the prerequisites of the ethic I have been describing. The resources that the Christian faith holds for living toward our dying in freedom and with hope and courage cannot be instantaneously transmitted to the sick person waiting upon death whose flesh already is ravaged and mind is tormented by disease. The meaning for living and dying which faith provides must be owned by the person over a lifetime.

At the risk of sounding self-contradictory, let me conclude that even as I believe that the church is the primary location of this ethic, the church's own special ministry of healing need not, indeed must not, be limited to believers.   There are people whose secular outlooks on medical ethics converge with the diagnoses, prescriptions, and prognoses of the church.   These people will see in limited but crucial ways the truth in Christian medical ethics. Others can be persuaded. Christian medical professionals who bring their faith into their practice can make a difference for sick people who do not believe in the God of Jewish and Christian scriptures.   I stand with the Presbyterian theologian William F. May that "it is pure angelism to assume that the sole witness of the church to the dying and the bereaved is the testimony of theology alone. A ministry to the flesh is a true and valid ministry" (May, 1987).   Biblical faith and Christian theology have a power to bring comfort and healing to persons outside the church. This I hold to be true because the Word assumed flesh, a flesh which all human beings share. We live and die as one humanity. The Son of God demonstrated this when he endured death for the salvation of all on the life-giving Cross.

References

May, William F. (1987).   The sacral power of death in contemporary experience. *On Moral Medicine,* eds. Stephen Lammers and Allen Verhey. Grand Rapids, Michigan: Wm. B. Eerdman's Pub. Co.: p. 181.

Schmemann, Alexander (1973). *For the Life of the World*, Crestwood, N.Y.: St. Vladimir's Seminary Press, p. 96.

Weiser, Benjamin (1991). A question of letting go. *Washington Post,* July 14, p. 1, 4.

Weiser, Benjamin (1991). While child suffered, beliefs clashed. *Washington Post,* July 15, p. 6

To Ease the Dying Process

John Breck

On October 23, 1991, Dr. Jack Kevorkian, a Michigan pathologist, provided the means by which two women ended their lives. Previously he had engaged in "physician-assisted suicide" in the case of Alzheimer's patient Janet Adkins. These persons were chronically ill but would not have been diagnosed as "terminal," that is, as having less than six months to live. Their deaths represented clear-cut examples of suicide, with the aim of ending what they considered to be the unbearable burden of their illness.

In an effort to sanction yet provide legal controls over medical intervention in such activity, right-to-die groups presented "Initiative 119" to the voters of Washington State on November 5, 1991. Although the Initiative was narrowly defeated, there is no doubt that its proponents and like-minded groups will continue to press for its most important and ominous provision: the legalization of physician-assisted suicide.

The Initiative contained three basic provisions. First, with reference to Washington's "Natural Death Act" that allows for Living Wills, it would have expanded the list of life-support technologies that a patient may refuse, to include feeding and hydration tubes. Second, it would have permitted the signer of a Living Will to stipulate that no life-support should be used if the person enters into a clinically diagnosable "persistent vegetative state" (PVS). These two modifications had been previously endorsed by the Washington State Medical Association. Opposed by the Association, and by many other religious and medical bodies, was the third provision. This would have allowed physician-assisted suicide of terminally ill patients on the basis of their written request, together with certification by at least two medical doctors that the patient has less than six months to live.[1] What is at issue here is the matter of "active euthanasia" or "mercy-killing."

Had the Initiative passed, it would have represented the world's first piece of enacted legislation to sanction direct euthanasia. Already "Sterbehilfe," physician-assisted suicide, is widely accepted and practiced in Holland and Germany, although it is not yet legally recognized. Its purpose is to assist through active medical intervention those who are diagnosed as terminally ill and, because of unmanageable pain or other severe physical or emotional distress, wish to end the protracted and burdensome process of dying.

Pressure for legislation to allow-- but more importantly, to regulate-- such practice is growing throughout virtually all industrialized societies today. Theologians as well as legislators are divided over the question. Although the issue may seem clear when examined in the light of Orthodox Tradition, its complexity and urgency require us to approach it with exceptional seriousness and sensitivity, in an effort to discern the will of God and to remain faithful to the guiding hand of His Spirit.

Passive Euthanasia

Both Roman Catholic and Orthodox ethicists today generally accept as morally "licit" a decision to remove life-support systems in terminal cases, when such removal clearly represents the desire of the patient and continued usage would serve no demonstrable good (McCormick, 1981 and Harakas, 1989). This point has been admirably made by Vigen Guroian in his paper, "Death, Euthanasia and Care for the Dying."[2] Confusion still exists, however, regarding precisely what means may be foregone in allowing the patient to die a "natural" death. Respirators, to most minds, represent "extraordinary means," and therefore they can be morally withdrawn. But what of feeding tubes, as the Washington Initiative proposed? Nutrition and hydration, after all, are basic requirements for sustaining life at any level, whether the organism is well or ill.

Nevertheless, many moral theologians are arguing today that removal of nasal-gastric tubes and IV-lines may be justifiable where a terminally ill patient has freely expressed the wish that no artificial means be sued to prolong his or her life. Although every person has what may be regarded as a natural "right" to food and water, in certain cases of terminal illness the procurement of such basic necessities is possible only through artificial means. In such cases, use of nasal-gastric tube would represent extraordinary medical intervention and could be refused. The actual cause of death would be attributable to the illness itself, rather than to the withholding or withdrawing of the tube.[3] While this may seem to some an illegitimate application of the principle of double effect, the morality of it seems to be confirmed by the observation that terminally ill patients often remove nasal-gastric tubes themselves, sensing that continued hydration only increases their physical distress in the later stages of the dying process. A growing number of reports from medical professionals who treat the terminally ill reinforce this conclusion. A recent survey, for example, indicated that eight out of ten hospice nurses agree that dehydration is actually beneficial to dying patients: it has the effect of creating natural body substance (keytones) that produce an analgesic effect. Moreover, it has been shown that continued hydration usually increases the level of pain and discomfort experienced by the terminally ill by complicating renal, pulmonary and gastrointestinal functions. (Rousseau, 1991).

The greatest hesitation with removing a nasal-gastric tube is due to the fear that the patient will suffer from starvation and dehydration. A conscious patient can make such discomfort known. In comatose or PVS patients, however, it must be clearly determined that neurological damage has rendered the person permanently insensate, before withholding or withdrawing nutrition and hydration can be considered either morally or medically appropriate. But once again, this presupposes that the patient has made known in advance his or her desire to refuse such treatment.

Another point needs to be made regarding "extraordinary" measures. Antibiotics are administered so routinely that they can hardly be considered anything but "ordinary." Yet their use has deprived terminally ill patients of a relatively simple and painless death by pneumonia. This long-respected "friend of the dying patient" no longer performs its vital function, and the terminally ill person is left to die by some other means-- means that can only be treated by extraordinary procedures. Yet what was extraordinary yesterday is routine today. The point is that we must guard assiduously against "vitalism": the bio-idolatry that holds that biological existence should be preserved at all cost. Respect for patient autonomy means respect for the dying process. When patients are diagnosed as terminally ill, and when they have stated in advance that no extraordinary means are to be used to prolong their life, they should have the option to refuse antibiotics as well. "Extraordinary procedures," then should be redefined as *any procedure that artificially prolongs the dying process*, and thereby deprives the patient of a "painless, blameless and peaceful" end to life.

Active Euthanasia

The Judeo-Christian tradition has consistently rejected arguments for direct or active euthanasia. The Washington Initiative would have permitted "adult persons with terminal conditions to request and receive aid-in-dying from their physicians, facilitating death."[5] Although the Initiative appears to offer a solution to the dying process out of a spirit of compassion, in fact it opens the door to incalculable abuse. The arguments against licensing doctors to kill have been put forth clearly and convincingly by the authors of the *Commonweal* Supplement of August 9, 1991. (Jonsen, et al, 1991). In this section I would simply add a few related remarks.

Christians, and particularly Orthodox Christians, rightly insist upon the redemptive quality of human suffering. To identify with the crucified Christ, in his own struggle and in that of his people, is fundamental to Christian existence. Yet we cannot for that reason hold that *all* suffering is by its very nature redemptive. In terminal cases particularly, physical pain and accompanying emotional anguish can in certain instances become unendurable and dehumanizing. Indeed, it is precisely this fact, illustrated by tragic cases of patients writhing in intractable pain, that leads so many people today to press for initiatives such as Washington State 119. The alternative is thus presented: dehumanize the medical profession by creating what Callahan calls "a new social institution-- private killing to relieve private suffering" (*Commonweal*, p. 14); or dehumanize the patient by subjecting him to the ravaging effects of terminal disease. This is, however, a false alternative, and needs to be acknowledged as such.

Advances in pain management have been hampered in this country by laws that prohibit certain drugs from being used medicinally. The most obvious of these is heroin. Because of the widespread, devastating use of street drugs, we are reluctant to consider measures that have become routine in other countries: use of the heroin or morphine-based "Brompton's cocktail,"[5] used so effectively in the St. Christopher hospices in England, for example, and other less addictive drugs such as marijuana. It is unreasonable to argue that drugs that are adequate for pain management may not be used in terminal cases because they are addictive.

By definition the terminally ill patient has less than six months to live. In cases of increasingly debilitating terminal disease (e.g., throat tumors, bone and colon cancer, advanced multiple sclerosis, AIDS), compassion and elementary respect for the dying person require that any and all available measures be used to relieve the pain that can lead to hopelessness and despair (that these are not hypothetical or even rare conditions is evident to anyone who spends a few hours in an emergency room or cancer ward . . . .). The dread of death is in many cases dread of the dying process and its attendant physical suffering. Adequate pain management, therefore, should be given the highest priority, to relieve the patient's anxiety and guarantee that his final days and hours be spent with a maximum of consciousness and minimum of physical distress.

Equally as important as improving techniques for pain management is the need to expand and develop *hospice programs* through the churches and various social agencies. A three-tiered hospice system has been inaugurated in this country, operating out of hospitals, in private homes, and in resident facilities which are usually open only to the terminally ill. As with hospital and home-care programs, these in-house facilities have proven highly effective in offering the compassionate, personal care and medical attention that can most adequately ease the dying process and provide a truly "good death," even to those who suffer potentially painful and debilitating illnesses. A sense of abandonment and loss of control over their lives is the gravest affliction experienced by most dying patients. The various forms of hospice care, if well administered, can relieve patients' anxiety by providing trained personnel to accompany them in their final journey and offer the emotional and spiritual support they crave.

A few Orthodox hospice programs exist in fledgling form, such as the St. Raphael's program sponsored by the Monastery of the Glorious Ascension in Resaca, Georgia, to serve persons afflicted with AIDS. These programs can provide an essential liturgical and sacramental setting, in which patient and priest together can seek healing through God's forgiving grace, even as the body nears death. Services of this kind should also be ranked as high priorities among the many pastoral tasks the church is called to assume. A monastic community can be an ideal setting in which to end one's earthly existence. But most communities are not equipped to offer the degree of care and comfort dying persons need. A new form of philanthropic organization, even a new expression of Christian vocation, seems required today, if the church is to provide a genuine alternative to physician-assisted suicide. True "aid-in-dying" could be furnished by specially trained Christian laypersons or medical professionals, who find themselves called to a vocation of service to the terminally ill.

There is a great deal of discussion within the Orthodox Church today about renewing the deaconate as a vocation of charitable *diakonia*. The suggestion has also been made that we create-- or rather, rediscover and reactivate-- the vocations of "deaconess," "virgin," and "widow." What better way to utilize the extraordinary yet sadly neglected gifts and capacities of Orthodox women, than to offer them the officially recognized and blessed opportunity to minister directly to those who are dying? While an "order of Sisters of Mercy," for example, would sound foreign to Orthodox ears, if it is carefully distinguished from the traditional monastic vocation and established as a pastoral ministry in its own right, such an order could provide the worthiest of services while enabling its members to undertake a thoroughly Christian ministry "in the world." And of course such a ministry need not be restricted to women, but could be open to anyone who wants to care for the sick and dying in a framework of nurture and prayer.

On a more modest level, our parishes could sponsor selected members of the community to be trained in hospice work, home-health-care, hospital visitation and the like. It is a well-known fact that as a patient approaches the terminal stage of life, doctors and other care providers tend to withdraw from them, leaving them with a desperate sense of abandonment. Care for the terminally ill is basically a *spiritual* task-- one that relies on appropriate medication, but acknowledges and accepts the inability of most medical teams to minister pastorally, spiritually, to those who no longer respond to their attempts to heal. It is the church's task to provide the loving care and nurture required to reconcile dying patients with God, family and friends, and to journey with them to the threshold of life beyond death. For our parishioners to assume this vital aspect of the church's ministry, however, they need a proper framework, with appropriate training and adequate funding. As difficult and utopian as this proposal might sound, experience has shown that a parish mobilized around an authentic *diakonia* can provide the material support that service requires. And such service offers its own reward by rejuvenating parish life through a renewed and living experience with the gospel of love.

Other and better suggestions can certainly be made. These few are proposed as initial steps, to counter the pressure now growing in American society for a "final solution" to the problem of the terminally ill. The church must reject active euthanasia. It can reasonably do so only by demonstrating through its actions and overall witness that there is indeed a better way.

Next Steps in the Debate

Where does this leave us relative to the increasingly loud demand for physician-assisted suicide?

Several critical issues raised here need a great deal of further study and debate among Orthodox ethicist and medical professionals. These include the following:

1. Withholding or withdrawing nasal-gastric tubes and IV-lines in terminal cases. Is such a decision morally acceptable, even on the grounds of prior instructions by the patient?

2. Should, as the Washington Initiative held, conditions such as irreversible coma and PVS be regarded as "terminal," thus potentially allowing the removal or refusal of life-sustaining measures, including nutrition and hydration?

3. To what degree is the practice of "snowing" morally justifiable (i.e., steadily increasing dosages of tranquilizers and analgesics with the intention of relieving pain, even though the medication will [as in the case of morphine] eventually depress the respiratory system and bring on death)?

4. How should Living Wills be worded and durable power of attorney be assigned, to guarantee appropriate care for the patient yet protect the care-givers from the ever-present specter of litigation?

5. How can the church educate her faithful appropriately to reshape attitudes long conditioned by "the American way of death"? How can we convey to our own and to the society about us, both the tragic nature of death and the truth of Christ's victory over this, the "last enemy"?

With regard to the Washington Initiative and the inevitable sequels it will spawn, we must affirm that physician-assisted suicide, euphemistically referred to as "aid-in-dying," is morally abhorrent and contrary to the will of God. To licence doctors to kill would undermine the medical profession and the need for patients to trust implicitly that their physician is there to heal; it would sanction suicide as an acceptable "way out" in virtually any circumstances; and it would create a system of basic inequality between those who can afford full medical coverage and thus life-prolonging care, and those who cannot. The real victims of legislation akin to Initiative 119 will be the poor, the abandoned, the mentally ill, and generally the marginalized members of our society. If ever the slippery slope posed an intolerable risk to personal and social welfare, it does so in the case of physician-assisted suicide.

This said, however, we need to justify our rejection of the practice by offering feasible and positive alternatives for the care of dying persons. As with the crisis of abortion, we cannot reject the solution of expediency unless we are willing to assume spiritual and material responsibility for the persons involved.

Above all, through the preaching and teaching of the church, we must convey the conviction that there is a greater value than sustained physical existence in a terminal state. The life freely bestowed by God must one day be freely and willingly surrendered to him, in order that he remain Lord over both the living and the dead. Our task is to find ever more compassionate and pastorally sound ways to accompany the dying toward the final step-- that they alone can take-- of surrendering their life and eternal destiny into the open, loving hands of God.

At the close of one of his Edifying Discourses, the Danish existentialist theologian Soren Kiekegaard spoke of this final step in words that appropriately describe the ultimate leap of faith: "So we may understand that the same God who by His hand led us through the world, now withdraws it, and opens his embrace to receive the longing soul." (Swenson, tr. 1943). For most people, the dying process involves at some point the sense that God has indeed withdrawn His hand, and the resulting sense of abandonment can lead them to hopelessness and despair. In such moments, suicide-- especially if it is physician assisted-- can seem both a reasonable and compassionate "way out." To preserve them from this final and most tragic temptation, we need to accompany the dying with compassion, love, and unshakable hope. And by our words and gestures, we need to convey to them the ultimate truth about death: that God's own deepest longing is precisely to open his embrace, to receive his dying child in a place of eternal rest, where sickness, sorrow and suffering are no more, but only the joy of life everlasting.

Notes

1 The official summary of the Initiative ran as follows: "This initiative expands the right of adult persons with terminal conditions to have their wishes, expressed in a written directive, regarding life respected. It amends current law to: expand the definition of terminal condition to include irreversible coma and persistent vegetative state or condition which will result in death within six months; specify which life-sustaining procedures may be withdrawn; permit adult persons with terminal conditions to request and receive aid-in-dying from their physicians, facilitating death." Quoted in A.R. Jonsen, "What is at Stake?" *Commonweal* (Supplement on Euthanasia: Washington State Initiative 119], August 9, 1991, p. 3.

2 "Euthanasia and Care for Dying in the Orthodox Tradition," delivered at the annual Orthodox Christian Association of Medicine, Psychology, and Religion conference held in Chicago on November 3, 1991. [The present volume, p. 35].

3 See R. McCormick, "Nutrition-Hydration: The New Euthanasia?," in *The Critical Calling. Reflections on Moral Dilemmas Since Vatican II* (Washington, D.C.: Georgetown University Press, 1989), p. 369-388; and T.A. Shannon, J.J. Walter, "The PVS Patient and the Forgoing/Withdrawing of Medical Nutrition and Hydration," in *Theological Studies* 49/4 (1988), 623-647. Compare the remarks of S.H. Wanzer and team, "The Physician's Responsibility Toward Hopelessly Ill Patients," *The New England Journal of Medicine*, vol. 310, no. 15 (April 12, 1984), 955-959, at 958: "*Patients in a persistent vegetative state.* In this state the neocortex is largely and irreversibly destroyed, although some brain-stem functions persist. When this neurologic condition has been established with a high degree of medical certainty and has been carefully documented, it is morally justifiable to withhold antibiotics and artificial nutrition and hydration, as well as other forms of life-sustaining treatment, allowing the patient to die. This

obviously requires careful efforts to obtain knowledge of the patient's prior wishes and the understanding and agreement of the family."

4 *See note 1.*

5 Developed for terminal illness therapy, the Brompton's cocktail is an alcohol solution with morphine or heroin, plus codeine and an optional tranquilizer. Its value lies in the fact that tolerance to it does not develop. In addition, it has been observed that patients who self-medicate with the cocktail require lower dosages than other patients, apparently because they are "in control." As the level of anxiety decreases, so does the level of perceived physical pain.

References

Breck, J. (1981). Selective non-treatment of the terminally ill. *St. Vladimir's Theological Quarterly*, 33/3, pp. 261-272.

Harakas, S. (1982). *Contemporary Moral Issues.* Minneapolis, Minnesota: Light and Life, pp. 170-173.

Jonsen, A.R. (1991).   What is at stake? *Commonweal* (Supplement on Euthanasia: Washington State Initiative 119) August .

McCormick, R. (1981). To save or let die: the dilemma of modern medicine, and (with R. Veatch), The preservation of life and self-determination. How Brave a New World? Dilemmas in Bioethics. Washington, D.C.: Georgetown University Press, pp. 339-351 and 381-389.

Rousseau, Paul C. M.D. (1991). How fluid deprivation affects the terminally ill. *RN*, January, pp. 73-76.

Swenson, tr. (1943). The expectation of faith. *Edifying Discourses I,* Minneapolis, Minnesota: Augsburg, p. 33.

Euthansia:
The Medical Encounter and Faith

John G. Demakis

The call came in the middle of the night. As a gynecology resident rotating through a large, private hospital, I had come to detest telephone calls, because invariably I would be up for several hours and would not feel good the next day. However, duty called, so I answered the phone. A nurse informed me that a patient was having difficulty getting rest, and asked if I could please see her. She was on Three North. That was the gynecologic-oncology unit, not my usual duty station. As I trudged along, bumping against walls and corners and not believing I was up again, I tried to imagine what I might find at the end of my walk. Maybe an elderly woman with an anxiety reaction, or perhaps something particularly horrible.

I grabbed the chart from the nurses station on my way to the patient's room, and the nurse gave me some hurried details: a twenty-year-old girl named Debbie was dying of ovarian cancer. She was having unrelenting vomiting apparently as the result of an alcohol drip administered for sedation. Hmmm, I thought. Very Sad. As I approached the room I could hear loud, labored breathing. I entered and saw an emaciated, dark-haired woman who appeared much older than twenty. She was receiving nasal oxygen, had an IV, and was sitting in bed suffering from what was obviously severe air hunger. The chart noted her weight at eighty pounds. A second woman, also dark-haired but of middle age, stood at her right, holding her hand. Both looked up as I entered. The room seemed filled with the patient's desperate effort to survive. Her eyes were hollow, and she had suprasternal and intercostal retractions with her rapid inspirations. She had not eaten or slept in two days. She had not responded to chemotherapy and had been given supportive care only. It was a gallows scene, a cruel mockery of her youth and unfulfilled potential. Her only words to me were, "Let's get this over with."

I retreated with my thoughts to the nurses station. The patient was tired and needed rest. I could not give her health, but I could give her rest. I asked the nurse to draw 20mg. of morphine sulfate into a syringe. Enough, I thought, to do the job. I took the syringe into the room and told the two women I was going to give Debbie something that would let her rest and for them to say good-bye. Debbie looked at the syringe, then laid her head on the pillow with her eyes open, watching what was left of the world. I injected the morphine intravenously and watched to see if my calculations would be correct. Within seconds her breathing slowed to a normal rate, her eyes closed, and her features softened as she seemed restful at last. The older woman stroked her hair. I waited for the inevitable next effect of depressing the respiratory drive. With clocklike certainty, within four minutes the breathing rate slowed even more, then became irregular, then ceased. The dark-haired woman stood erect and seemed relieved. "It's over, Debbie." (Anonymous, 1988).

The above article appeared in the *Journal of the American Medical Association* (*JAMA*) in 1988 and galvanized the medical community. Never in an American medical journal had a case of active euthanasia been reported. The article appeared without an author's name-- another first for the *JAMA*. A storm of protest flooded the journal from physicians deploring the article and from states attorneys demanding to know the name of the physician. Since this pivotal article, euthanasia has been discussed in the medical and lay literature with increasing frequency. In addition, the national news media has reported two more suicides assisted by Dr. Kevorkian and his suicide machine. With this heightened awareness and the ethical issues it raises, it is fitting that OCAMPR examine the issue of euthanasia.

The four questions to be addressed are:

1) Should euthanasia be allowed?
2) Do the dying need alternatives?
3) Is euthanasia ever justified? and

4) Who should decide if and when someone should die?

I will try to give my perspective of the problem as an Orthodox Christian physician who has had the opportunity and the honor to treat many dying patients. I hope in the process to give you some insight into the above questions.

First, I will define some commonly used terms that are often misunderstood. It is critical to our discussions to agree upon definitions for certain terms:

A. Euthanasia. Allowing a patient to die when he, or she could be kept alive with appropriate medical procedures (e.g. life support is never started or where life support is terminated). Passive euthanasia may be with or without the patient's consent. In effect, passive euthanasia allows nature to take its course.

B. Active Euthanasia. A direct attempt to terminate life, usually by drug administration. Active euthanasia may be:

1. With the patient's consent-- aiding in suicide (mercy killing). This is illegal in 27 states. In no state is it legal.
2. Without the patient's consent-- murder.

C. Brain Dead Patients. Total absence of brain waves on an Electroencephalogram (EEG) as documented by a board certified neurologist. Many states now have statutes that enable physicians to pronounce the patient dead who has absent brain waves and to remove life support systems. This definition is unambiguous and easily determined. No one has ever recovered consciousness who was brain dead. Indeed, even with life support these patients do not live very long-- several weeks usually. The statutes consider these patients as dead. According to such an understanding, life support is removed not to allow the patient to die, but because the patient is already dead treatment can be stopped.

E. Persistent Vegetative State. Patient has no cortical brain waves, only scattered brain waves from lower brain centers on the EEG as read by a neurologist. In these cases, the patient has suffered partial but not total brain destruction. The President's Commission for the Study of Ethical Problems in Medicine and Biomedical and Behavioral Research has defined the vegetative state as follows: "Personality, memory, purposeful action, social interaction, sentience, thought and even emotional states are gone. Only vegetative functions and reflexes persist. If food is supplied, the digestive system functions and controlled evacuation occurs; the kidneys produce urine, the heart, lung and blood vessels continue to move air and blood; and nutrients are distributed in the body. (Presidential Commission, 1983).

Since the lower brain centers are still intact, when life support is terminated in such a patient, he or she may continue to breath, and, if properly fed, may live many years (as in Karen Quinlan) in the vegetative state. Have any patients ever recovered from this state? Only a few have regained consciousness. However, in the words of the Presidential Commission, "The few patients who have regained consciousness after a prolonged period of unconsciousness were severely disabled. The degree of permanent damage varied but commonly included inability to speak or see, permanent distortion of the limbs or paralysis . . . Thus even the extremely small likelihood of "recovery" cannot be compared with returning to a normal or relatively well functioning state." (Presidential Commission, 1983, pp.182-183).

F. Difference of Brain Dead and Persistent Vegetative State

1. The brain dead individual cannot breathe independently but requires ventilator support, whereas the individual in a persistent vegetative state can survive without a ventilator.

2. The brain dead individual will expire shortly (typically within a week or two) despite our best efforts, whereas the individual in a persistent vegetative state can, by virtue of artificial feeding, be kept alive for years.

Passive Euthanasia

The cases of Karen Quinlan and Nancy Cruzan have helped define many of the legal issues concerning passive euthanasia. Karen Quinlan of New Jersey and Nancy Cruzan of Missouri were two young women in vegetative states whose families were involved in long court battles. Judges in both cases eventually granted the families requests to terminate life support. These two cases were highly publicized and helped to set present guidelines concerning passive euthanasia-- especially in terminating life support.

A much publicized Chicago case involved Rudy Linares, a father who held medical staff and police at bay with a gun as he disconnected his fifteen-month-old comatose son's life support at Presbyterian-St. Luke's Hospital and held him in his arms until he died. He was allowed to plead guilty on misdemeanor charges and was released on probation.

Illinois recently passed one of the most detailed laws concerning termination of life support. Under the Illinois law, hospitals no longer have to go to court to terminate respirators or feeding tubes. Patients must be incurable, irreversibly and terminally ill and have no advanced directives.

Passive euthanasia usually occurs in patients who are brain dead or in a persistent vegetative state. Most states have passed statutes regulating passive euthanasia. Although there are differences, most states allow life support to be terminated in brain dead or the persistent vegetative states if the patient has an advanced directive (living will) or if the next of kin agree to it. Where there is no advanced directive and no next of kin many states spell out how a physician can request to terminate life support.

These are the legal issues in passive euthanasia. What is our Church's position? Many may not be aware of the excellent medical facilities that were developed in the Byzantine Christian Empire. Indeed, the Byzantines were the first to develop hospitals as we know them today. Every major city had a full array of medical facilities incuding hospitals, nursing homes and hospices. The Orthodox Church was fully involved in all philanthropic institutions in the Byzantine Empire. In fact, physicians were often monks or priests or both. Here is an example of how a terminally ill patient was treated. I quote from the excellent book by Timothy Miller, *The Birth of the Hospital in the Byzantine Empire*:

> In the 10th century in the Euboulos Xenon, in Constantinople, a case is described where the physicians treated a very difficult case for seven days. At the end of that time, the doctors decided that the patient could not recover. They ceased treatment and had the patient removed from the xenon proper to a nearby hostel so that a new patient could be admitted. But the xenon observed Christian philanthropia by continuing to feed and house the dying man in a separate facility. (Miller, 1985).

Today, passive euthanasia is well accepted legally and by most religions. Fr. Harakas, in his most informative book, *For the Health of the Body and Soul*, states, "When, especially, there is no evidence of brain activity in the conjunction with the systemic breakdown, we can safely say that the patient is no longer alive in any religiously significant way, and that, in fact, only certain organs are functioning. In such a case there is no moral responsibility to continue the use of artificial means." (Harakas, 1980). He goes on to mention a whole service in the Prayerbook of the Eastern Orthodox Church devoted to those in the process of dying. The term used is "struggling to die," which is a very appropriate term. The prayer asks God to separate the soul from the body, thus giving rest to the dying person.

In summary, I believe that passive euthanasia in brain dead or in patients in a persistent vegetative state is appropriate, both legally and morally. I believe this because I do not believe the patient is alive in the Christian understanding of life.

Active Euthanasia

I have already defined active euthanasia. What types of patients ask for active euthanasia? Well, first they are not brain dead or in a persistent vegetative state. They would not need active euthanasia. Rather, they are patients who are awake, alert and in full control of their faculties. Some patients who have asked assistance in committing suicide are:

A. **Patients with terminal illness.** Patients with a terminal illness who may or may not be suffering from severe pain or other severe symptoms.
B. **Patients with non-terminal illness.** Patients with non-terminal illness, but with severe symptoms or disability (severe pain, multiple sclerosis, Alzheimer's, etc.).

One to two years ago, any discussion on euthanasia would have been primarily concerned with passive euthansia. Active euthanasia would hardly be discussed. However, today, it is one of the most talked about issues in our society. There is even a book on the best-sellers list for several weeks now giving detailed instructions to patients and physicians on how to commit suicide and how to aid a patient to commit suicide. It is a very troubling book (Humphry, 1991). Mr. Humphry of the Hemlock Society goes into great detail about how to commit suicide including specific doses of drugs to use and other minute details.

In addition, our society has been galvanized by Dr. Jack Kevorkian and his suicide machine-- which was in the national media almost continously for some time. To put active euthanasia in perspective, let us examine how physicians have looked at it through the ages.

First, let us look at the Hippocratic Oath-- the traditional oath taken by all medical students at their graduation:

> I will neither give a deadly drug to anybody if asked for it, nor will I make a suggestion to this effect. Similarly, I will not give to any woman an abortive remedy. In purity and holiness I will guard my life and my art. (Edelstein, 1943).

Physician participation in suicide and abortion was common in ancient Greece and Rome. It was accepted by all of the philosophical schools except the Pythagorean School. The Hippocratic Oath stands out as an exception in ancient times. The oath was not popular in ancient times and only came into use after the start of the Christian era. It was used in all medical schools worldwide until the last twenty years when a new form of oath was taken, usually omitting references to the gods, euthanasia, and abortion.

Presently, 27 states ban assisted suicide. No state has legalized assisted suicide. However, the voters in the state of Washington were asked to make theirs the first political jurisdiction in the world to legalize active euthanasia. The citizens of the state of Washington subsequently defeated Initiative 119 which would have made "aid-in-dying" a medical service that doctors could perform at the request of terminally ill patients.[1]

The case of Dr. Kevorkian, "Dr. Death", and his suicide machine, was well publicized because of two suicides in which he assisted. Neither patient was terminal. One suffered from multiple sclerosis and the other severe abdominal pain. The lady with multiple sclerosis stated, "I'm like a 42 year-old baby. I have to be clothed, fed and taken care of. Suicide is not a new thought. It is a ten-year thought. I should have done something a long time ago when I was capable." The lady with severe abdominal pain was quoted as saying, "After three and a half years, I cannot go on with this pain and agony. No doctor can help me anymore. If God won't come to me, I'm going to find God."

Many patients contemplating suicide have severe depression that needs to be diagnosed and treated. The medical profession often is slow to diagnose depression in a patient with a significant medical condition. Yet both of Dr. Kevorkian's patients, from their brief statements, may very well have been depressed. How tragic if they were not offered psychiatric help. Every such patient should be carefully evaluated for depression and offered treatment if necessary.

I believe that active euthanasia is morally wrong. I do not believe physicians should participate in patient suicide. It violates our solemn oath to do our best for the patient. I also strongly believe that physicians who participate in patient suicide will also harm themselves. For every such act they commit they will further inure themselves to a patient's death and it will become easier and easier for them to kill. I would hope no young medical student or physician reads the book *Final Exit*. What a horrible way to begin their healing career.

The Role of Church and Active Euthanasia

The Church has always been against suicide and active euthanasia.

Although I agree with these positions, the proponents of active euthanasia (especially for mercy killing), present important arguments that must be addressed. Terminal patients or patients with severe pain or disability can have a difficult life, full of pain and discomfort. A life that is so caught up with their pain that they can have no rest and can think of nothing else. The point is made that if this condition is irreversible, there is no futher dignity or usefulness to that life.

The Church has always condemned this approach. Life is a gift of God and we cannot decide when it should cease. Even the suffering can be helpful (Harakas, 1980). It is even pointed out that spiritual growth can take place through suffering, quoting Romans 8:17-39. As a whole, most churches have condemned active euthanasia as violating the sanctity of life.

Most physicians, I believe, agree with this position. However, they also understand that patients who are contemplating suicide are often "at the end of their rope." They are in such distress from pain, vomitting, or other severe symptoms, that they cannot think clearly or for that matter, participate in their spiritual struggle. They often feel they are a burden to society or their families. They feel alone, abondoned and unable to serve any useful purpose.

It is not enough for the Church to condemn active euthanasia and assisted suicide. The Church must lead in the effort to give dignity to their lives by showing them that they are important and have a useful function in this life. That useful function could be to allow others to care for them and thus demonstrate their Christian love and caring. And by thus showing their Christian love, these caring people grow toward their own goal of *theosis*. Mother Teresa in Calcutta does exactly this. If we were to ask anyone today if there is a saint onthis earth, the most frequent name mentionsed would be Mother Teresa. What does she do? She cares for the sick and dying. It is interesting, that during the Byzantine Empire the Church and State sponsored many hospices for the dying. Do we have any today? Where are our Church's programs today to help these poor suffering people?

Our Church needs to develop hospices,[2] home care programs[3] or other such programs that will tend to the needs of these unfortunate people. We must encourage our people to reach out to those who are suffering and to their families. By showing our love and concern for these people the Church will give them dignity and understanding that they are not alone and abondoned. Hopefully this will encourage them to carry on and to accept God's will. They will also give the Church the opportunity to practice Christian love.

The churches should work closely with the medical profession to operate the above type of facilities. Just by visiting and caring we can help the patient and their families while the patient "struggles to die." I believe it is imperative for the Church to take a lead in helping such patients. They are in desperate situations. They do not need moralizing, rather, they need care and concern. What better way for the Church to fulfill its mission to these unfortuante people and to their families?

Notes

[1] The measure was defeated.

[2] Hospices are special facilities usually associated with hospitals but have separate wings. They are usually staffed with doctors, nurses, social workers and priests or ministers who are experience in working with dying patients. A hospice is not a place to get well but a place to die. It is for patients with terminal illnesses. Patients who go there know they are going to die. The staff is experienced in making patients comfortable. There is no attempt at

resuscitation when the heart stops. Pain control is an important feature. There is often a fine line between freedom from pain and mental confusion. These people are experts at it. Special regimens have been developed for pain control, control of nausea and vomitting (which can be very debilitating in the dying patient), control of constipation, shortness of breath and other symptoms that often make dying patients so uncomfortable that their last days or hours on earth can be sheer torture.

3 Hospital-Based Home Care allows patients who are dying to spend most of their last days and hours at home, if they have appropriate care-givers at home. This program will send nurses, doctors, and other health professionals into the home to help and support the actual care-givers which are usually the spouse or children of the dying patient. Family members are taught how to give injections, change catheters, manage pain medications, etc. If the family knows they have the support of the health professionals, it is amazing what they can do. They can call a hospital number and someone will always be on duty 24 hours a day to answer questions, offer support, or visit the home. There are many other programs that have been developed for the same purpose. They usually have some of the above features. Each will have something unique. Some are church-based, some are community-based.

References

Anonymous, (1988). *Journal of the American Medical Association*, edited by Roxanne K. Young. American Medical Association, 259, no. 2, January 8, p. 272.

Edelstein, Ludwig (1943). *The Hippocratic Oath*. Ares Publishers.

Harakas, Stanley S. (1980). *For the Health of the Body and Soul, An Eastern Orthodox Introduction to Bioethics*. Brookline, Massachusetts: Holy Cross Orthodox Press, p. 37.

Humphry, Derek (1991). *Final Exit-- The Practicalities of Self-Deliverance and Assisted Suicide for the Dying*. The Hemlock Society.

Miller, Timothy S. (1985). *The Birth of the Hospital in the Byzantine Empire*. John Hopkins University Press, p. 213.

Presidential Commission (1983). Deciding to forego life-sustaining treatment: A report of the ethical, medical, and legal issues in treatment decisions. *The President's Commission for the Sudy of Ethical Problems in Medicine and Biomedical and Behavioral Research*, Washington: GPO, pp. 174-175.

PART III

Decisions Near the End of Life

In modern times, the spiritual meaning of death for Orthodox Christians is not only directed to medical issues but it is also thrust into the legal sphere. This paper addresses decisions concerning health care providers involving the decisions of life support and resuscitation in view of the living will.

A gathering of physicians and religious leaders concerning this topic produced a concensus of guidelines, for an Orthodox Christian perspective, concerning the development of a living will as recommendations for "helping professionals" and the laity about health and faith.

Decisions Near the End of Life: A Living Will and a Christian Death

Monk Ioannikios
Maurice L. Sill
Peter Bushunow, M.D.
John G. Demakis, M.D.
John Johnstone, M.D.
Dismas Kriegel

This paper is an attempt to state the consensus from and discussions and correspondence among the authors about decisions near the end of life. One person who shared in part of this discussion is now the widow of a recent victim of terminal cancer. Her late husband went through a period of dying that was painful and agonizing, but also challenging and soul-searching. She wrote a very touching letter saying that while the questions are very difficult, it is a great consolation to know the Church is not indifferent but is sharing in the search for the right response to often unprecedented and heart-rending decisions.

The Challenge

The hour of death is a critical moment in our lives as Christians. Scripture says the very memory of it can keep us from sin (Wisdom of Jesus).

As rational sheep of Christ's little flock who are also members of modern American society, we must clarify in our minds what we anticipate in response to our continuous prayer to God for a Christian end to our life. This means confronting problems which are new and perhaps unique to our generation.

In this paper we will discuss making decisions about health care procedures called life support and resuscitation. These procedures seek to prolong a patient's life when he is expected to die without them.

In a recent book, *Strangers at the Bedside*, David J. Rothman documents how a group of outsiders, lawyers, legislators, judges, and even accountants have come to clog the space around the patient's hospital bed, revolutionizing the control of medical decision making (Eppinger, 1991).

Along with medical personnel, health care administrators, the courts and ethicists, the government is also involving itself more and more in the way we die through bureaucratic review of medical care and costs as well as increased litigation and legislation.

As our society becomes more and more legalistic, one reaction has been to provide a valid legal document which expresses a person's wishes about dying. Several states have passed laws providing for living wills, durable powers of attorney or other advance directives, such as the request "Do not resuscitate."

As Orthodox Christians we are faced with the challenge of defining our convictions concerning death in this context. We must look critically at living wills and their implications to see whether or not they are suitable for our use. Orthodox Christian clergy and laymen must cooperate with the professionals in responding to the needs of the dying and of their loved ones.

Defining Death

For the Orthodox Christian, death is a great mystery. We can define certain boundaries outside which understandings of this mystery are not in harmony with the divine revelation of saving truth, which is treasured in the Church. While it is humanly impossible to define exactly "what it is," we often call it the separation of the soul from the body.

The courts and medical science require a neurophysiological criterion to determine when a person is legally dead. Their technical criterion for establishing the fact of physical death must not be confused with moral, philosophical and religious concepts of death. We accept an externally observable criterion which satisfies the legitimate needs of the medical and legal communities as long as it does not encroach on the providence of the Church.

The most widely accepted criterion at present is the cessation of brainstem activity as registered on the electroencephalogram. No patient has been known to survive without brainstem waves, and other vital functions usually cease within minutes of life support termination. Resuscitation procedures can start heart beat and breathing in many instances; no procedure is known at present for restarting brain activity.

It has been noted that this definition is a double compromise. First it is a compromise "with a concept of death as complete disintegration of the human organism's biological functioning, with all living components dead or at least totally disintegrated and dissociated from each other." (Gillon, 1990).

Certain vital organs may still be functioning after the determination of brain death. This compromise makes such organs available for transplant. By defining the end of the death process as the cessation or absence of brainstem activity, it bypasses the sinister overtones of such a statement as this:

> The transplant procedure will end the death process but will not constitute the cause of the donor's death. (Rix, 1990).
>
> On the other hand, brain death criteria are also a compromise with the concept of death understood as cessation of personal existence, for brain death criteria will classify as alive some humans who are dead as persons. (Gillon, 1990).

This last statement involves philosophical judgements we must question. Must a human being have a capacity for consciousness in order to be considered a person? What about the newly conceived human zygote? Court rulings on abortion show what can happen when a human being ceases to be viewed as a legal person.

When a patient shows brainstem activity but an absence of cortical brain waves he is said to be in a vegetative state. In many cases, there may be little reason to expect such a person to regain consciousness.

However, note the use of the word *persistent* rather that such terms as *permanent* and *irreversible* which exclude the unexpected and extraordinary, not to say the miraculous. The inference that an unconscious or comatose patient has become a "vegetable" is disquieting.

Fr. Harakas points out that for the Church, the patient in such a state is "struggling to die"; this person is in critical need of special prayers and spiritual help. (Harakas, 1980).

Complications

In an editorial on the Patient Self Determination Act passed by Congress in 1990, the *Journal of the American Medical Association* comments:

> The law requires Medicare/Medicaid-receiving health care providers to inform patients of their existing rights under state law to refuse treatment and prepare advance directives . . . It is probably safe to say that in recent years a good many of the health care regulations that have come from federal sources have had cost containment as their major, if not primary, goal. The ethical concern is certainly not cost containment per se, but the danger that institutional financial considerations will constitute some form of 'undue influence' or subtle coercion applied to patients or their families to limit care inappropriately. This concern is well founded . . . (White, 1991).1

The results of some relevant studies were cited in the same journal.

> Considerable reservations have been raised about the meaning, reliability, durability, and portability of living wills. In one study, 13% of 65 nursing home residents who had advance directives limiting their care changed their decisions in favor of more care, although another study showed that most hospitalized patients' preferences remained stable for a month after their transfer from an intensive care unit. In a recent work, the presence of an advance directive did not increase the likelihood that patients' wishes would be followed. Indeed, in 25 of 71 cases, the advance directive did not make it to the patient's hospital chart when the patient was transferred from nursing home to hospital. (La Puma, et al, 1991).

Concerning instruments entrusting decisions to other persons or proxies, it has been found that:

Problems such as emotional burden, impending divorce, and financial motivations have prompted proxies to misrepresent patient wishes. Disagreement among family members about patient care are common and often the subject of ethics consultation. At least seven studies show that potential proxy decision makers often do not know whether patients wish to have life-sustaining treatment, including intensive care, cardiopulmonary resuscitation and cardiovascular surgery. Proxies are often uncertain of whether patients are satisfied with their current care and tend to underestimate elderly outpatients' quality of life. (La Puma, et al, 1991).

In the celebrated Cruzon case the decision of the Supreme Court of the United States was ignored by the local judge who granted the parents' request to terminate life-sustaining procedures.   Attorney Kriegel comments:

> By that time, the Missouri Attorney General's office had broken off its involvement in the matter for reasons completely political. Since there was no one left with 'standing' available to appeal the improper order, and since the parents certainly had what they wanted, the girl's nutrition and hydration, as it's put, were terminated and death ensued from starvation and lack of water." (Kriegle, 1991).

The standard form of a living will states a person's decision to refuse "unduly prolonging the dying process," while requesting medication and other procedures providing for pain relief and comfort.

There are many questions about "how to interpret inflexible, vague documents such as living wills" and "patients' rights under the laws of their state may be less than their rights under the United States Constitution" (La Puma, et al, 1991). Judge Welliver of the Supreme Court of Missouri wrote in his dissent on the Cruzon case,

> The opinion unnecessarily and by dictum seeks to place a mantle of constitutionality on the Missouri Living Will Statute, which statute in my opinion has been a fraud on the people of Missouri from the beginning and which statute, if directly attacked, must, in my opinion, be held to be unconstitutional.

Thus, the execution of a living will is by no means guaranteed by the very medical and legal community which encourages a person to draw up such a document. Many cross currents in the winds of change are eroding concepts we used to take for granted regarding doctors, lawyers and death. As in the case with abortion, we may see laws enacted which are contrary to the law of Christ.

Responsibilities

Many decisions cannot be foreseen and predetermined in a legal document, whether it be a living will drawn up in advance or a standard form signed along with other papers on admission to a health care facility. Understanding and support must be provided for those close to us through the sympathetic cooperation of medical professionals with our spiritual father or pastor. This requires forethought as well as God's help in the hour of need.

When a patient consults the medical profession, he initiates a relationship which has now come under close scrutiny. Patients are becoming more and more assertive in deciding what the professionals will do to them. The medical community, on its part, is becoming increasingly holistic and sensitive not only in attempting to restore a patients' health but also to help the terminally ill to die.

We should not wait until we land in the Intensive Care Unit with a terminal condition to prepare for death. We may be unconscious or otherwise incapable of making crucial decisions if we do. The invitation to verbalize our wishes is in full accord with Christian preparation for death, for our departure into eternity.

Some studies show that persons who have made living wills or advance directives find some comfort in them, show less anxiety about dying and greater inner control (La Puma, et al, 1991). We would suggest that it may be the other way around. The listed qualities may characterize persons willing to face and make these decisions in advance.

Pastors and concerned laymen should initiate discussion and serious consideration of the issues a person who dies in modern America is likely to confront. Such discussion should involve pastoral guidance for the entire family as well as appropriate professionals and friends.

Pastoral support and guidance is especially needed in times of crisis. The Orthodox pastor should be prepared but an active and informed layman can also play a key role, be he a health care employee, a relative, a friend or simply a concerned fellow Christian.

The needs are many: explaining the technical language of a document to a person asked to sign, bridging language and cultural barriers, in addition to providing a sympathetic and trustworthy presence at a time of critical need.

Another area for creative cooperation between the medical professionals, pastors and laymen lies in exploring the many and varied alternatives in preventing illnesses, in treating them and in caring for the dying. Medical professionals are now trained and expected to be sensitive to a dying patient's needs. Orthodox clergy should be prepared to assist both them and the patients in meeting these needs. The concerned layman may provide the opportunity for them to consult and work together.

In other words, there is a contemporary summons for us to express our faith actively. A living will seeks to provide for one set of circumstances. But a process is involved, not just a document, in preparing in advance consciously and conscientiously for a Christian end to our life.

Criteria

SS. Dositheos and Seraphim both refused medical intervention; the former died while the latter was miraculously healed. Many holy fathers humbly submitted to their doctors and a number of them, such as the Holy Unmercenaries, were themselves members of the medical profession. Other saints, however, preferred to endure their afflictions and denied themselves medical care along with other things of this world; they delighted in the voluntary sufferings they endured for the sake of Christ.

What criteria underlie the actions of these saints? Reacting to attempts to define "good" and "bad" medicine (such as "natural" and "unnatural"), one of us observed that the medicines themselves are neither good nor bad; they are put to either good or bad use.

For the medical profession the criterion for deciding whether a procedure is being put to "good" or "bad" use is based on whether it benefits or harms the patient's health. In Orthodoxy, the ultimate criterion must be a "Christian end to our life" insofar as our human efforts are brought to fruition by God's grace and providence.

The icon of the Dormition of the Theotokos expresses this mystery most eloquently. Surrounded by the saints and angels, the Most Holy Mother of God has painlessly surrendered her spirit into the hands of her Son and God; her soul, newly born in eternity, is lovingly born up in His arms.

There are many accounts of simple righteous people who understood when they were going to die and who passed away into eternal rest quite painlessly after communing the Holy Mysteries. Here we find the same ideal: the prayerful surrender of one's soul into the hands of Christ.

Yet many saints, including all the holy martyrs and even our Savior Himself, died amid excruciating physical torment. The face of the crucified Christ in Orthodox iconography does not show agony, however, but peace and humble submission. In spite of physical pain and suffering, their souls were filled with consolation and their death was "painless."

We pray for "a Christian end to our life, painless, blameless and a good defence before the dreadful judgement Seat of Christ." This means attaining peace of conscience through confession, repentance, and forgiveness of sins, by reconciliation and communion with Christ in prayer and the Holy Mysteries.

Every individual is different both in life and in death, and God provides for each individual in a particular and special way. In many instances the dying process transforms a person completely and loved ones as well.

The suffering of the dying requires more than pain relief; it is an opportunity for spiritual growth. The pastor and loved ones should share in this growth as they care for the dying. The Cross and Golgotha lead to the Resurrection. The Orthodox Church offers special care for the dying. Communion of the Holy Mysteries together with confession forms the essential core; there are special services for the dying and also specific prayers for those "struggling to die."

Persons who are incommunicative or unconscious may be experiencing an intense spiritual crisis. There are numberless accounts of unexpected turns of events that made dying persons able or unable to confess and receive Holy Communion.

In departing from this life our attention must be focused on the eternal life we will be entering, on the spiritual health of our soul as our body ceases to function. The Christian does not face death alone. The pastor, health care professionals, family and friends, the parish community together with the entire Church both visible and invisible have a vital role to perform in providing a Christian end to our life.

Check List

In summary, we submit the following list of important points which may be helpful for the pastor, medical professional and layman initiating the kind of interpersonal process and developing the relationships needed for suitable decision-making regarding our preparation for death:

1. As Orthodox Christians we view death as a crucial moment in our religious life and therefore wish above all to provide for our spiritual needs.

2. In advance we should select a doctor who understands and respects our convictions and we should initiate discussions with him concerning them.

3. Because we feel a moral responsibility to care for our bodies, we seek the support of the medical profession in preventing illnesses and avoiding habits, foods, medicines, etc., which may endanger our health. We also expect to be informed about the side effects of drugs prescribed to us, about dietary rules we should follow when taking medication, and alternative methods of treatment.

4. We assert our right to request second opinions and to seek other forms of health care and to make our own choices concerning them.

5. We wish to be informed concerning any condition or illness which may be terminal.

6. In the event of a crisis, our pastor or spiritual father must be informed immediately so that he can provide for our spiritual needs. If we have a doctor who understands our wishes, we can direct that he participate in all major decisions regarding our treatment. We should discuss these matters with persons close to us so they will know what to do in case of any emergency.

7. We wish to be lucid and free from mind-effecting medication in order to make a good confession, to pray, receive Holy Communion and consciously prepare for death. Medical provision for our comfort and pain relief as well as life support should be administered with this in constant consideration.

8. We reject any form of euthanasia, assisted suicide, or any procedures which involve the occult or procedures which are contrary to the teachings of the Orthodox Church.

9. Any decision about the termination of life support or the refusal of medical intervention must be made by persons whom we specify. If our close relatives do not share our convictions, we can draw up a legal document entrusting such decisions to persons whom we trust and who know and understand our convictions and wishes. Our pastor and doctor should know about any such document and its contents.

10. We believe in the sanctity of life but do not fear death. We believe God provides for each person at the hour of death. We therefore direct that every opportunity be given for our pastor to administer Confession and Holy Communion and to assist us with the prayers and rites of the Orthodox Church even if our loss of consciousness seems to be irreversible. On the other hand, we reserve the right to refuse any medical intervention which we feel would interfere with our spiritual preparation for death.

Times and customs change. Orthodox Christians have always faced death as members of Christ with the pledge of eternal life. This is exactly what we must learn to do in our day and age just as our forefathers learned in the course of their earthly and spiritual lives.

We conclude with some relevant sayings from the Holy Fathers:

Words of Wisdom

"God makes the earth yield healing herbs which the prudent man should not neglect; was not the water sweetened by a twig that man might learn His power? He endows man with the knowledge to glory in His mighty works, through which the doctor eases pain and the druggist prepares his medicines . . . My son, when you are ill, delay not, but pray to God, who will heal you . . . Then give the doctor his place . . . for you need him too . . . and he too beseeches God that his diagnosis may be correct and his treatment bring about a cure."

Sirach 38:1-15 [2]

"Medicine is an example of what God allows men to do when they work in harmony with Him and with one another."

St. Gregory of Nyssa [3]

"God's grace is as evident in the healing power of medicine and its practitioners as it is in miraculous cures."

St. Basil the Great [4]

"Because God gave them [physicians] a special talent to save others from pain and sometimes death, they have an urgent responsibility to share their talents."

St. John Chrysostom [5]

"In Caesarea I felt much better and more at ease, because here I made use of the medicines and advice of the very best and most famous physicians who treated me not only with medicine but much more with sympathy and friendship towards me."

St. John Chrysostom [6]

"When you fall ill, put all hope of recovery in God and entreat Him with reverence and humility. But also do not neglect what is in your power; summon a physician, keep a diet, take medicine, do not reject treatment. God is both the physician for your illness and the one who grants you health. But He grants you health and life only when you do not reject what you need for your recovery. This is what King Hezekiah did. He hoped in God that he would receive from Him healing of his illness and be beseeched Him with many fervent tears for both life and health. However, he did not refuse to grind up figs and place the plaster made from them on his boil, on the advice of the Prophet Isaiah who told him: 'Let them take a lump of figs and lay it for a plaster upon the boil, and he shall recover' (Is 38:21)."

Nicephorus Theotokos, Archbishop of Astrakhan [7]

"He that sins against his Creator falls into the hands of the physician" (Sir 38:15). "That is, he submits to the treatments of the doctors as it were as chastisement for his sins, for illnesses are the result of sin."

Elder Hilarion of Optina [8]

"It must be said that many times God permits the virtuous to be tempted . . . He allows many evils to rise against them from every side. He smites them in their bodies, like Job, and brings them to poverty, causes them to be repudiated by mankind, and strikes them in whatever they possess; their souls alone are not approached by harm. For it is not possible, when we are faring on the way of righteousness, for us not to encounter gloom, and for the body not to travail in sickness and pains, and to remain unaltered, if indeed our love is to live in virtue. But the man who of his own will lends himself to the slaying or the destruction of his own life or to anything else that is harmful, is under condemnation."

St. Isaac of Syria [9]

"Let us then not tremble at death. Our soul hath by nature the love of life, but it lies with us either to loose the bands of nature, and make this desire weak; or else to tighten them, and make the desire more tyrannous. For just as we have the desire for sexual intercourse, but when we practice true wisdom we render the desire weak, so also with regard to life. God has joined carnal desire to the generation of children, to maintain a succession among us, without however forbidding us from traveling the higher road of continence; likewise He has implanted in us the love of life, forbidding us from destroying ourselves, but not hindering our despising the present life. And it behooves us, knowing this, to observe due measure, and neither to go at any time to death of our own accord, even though ten thousand terrible things possess us; nor yet, when dragged to it, for the sake of what is pleasing to God, to shrink back and fear it, but boldly to strip for it, preferring the future to the present life."

St. John Chrysostom [10]

"Do not despond in the time of violent temptations, affliction, or sicknesses, or at obstacles arising from the disturbance of the enemy; all this is the reproof and chastisement of the righteous Lord, Who trieth the hearts and reins, for your cleansing, arousing, and correction, for burning out the thorns of carnal passions. And therefore do not complain if you sometimes suffer greatly. Do not think of the suffering, but of the blessed consequences for this chastisement, and the health of the soul. What would you not do for the health of your body? Still more must you bear everything for the health and salvation of your soul, which has eternal life."

St. John of Kronstadt [11]

Notes

[1]   See also John Johnstone's "The Coming Holocaust of the Aged," *The Physician Alert*, vol. 5, no. 11.

[2]   Wisdom of Jesus, Son of Sirach 38: 1-15.

3 St. Gregory of Nyssa, *Pauperibus*, p. 12.

4 St. Basil the Great, *Regulae Fustus Tractatus*, Interrogatio 55, PG, 31:1044-52.

5 St. John Chrysostom, *De Perfecta Charitate*, PG, 56: 279-80.

6 St. John Chrysostom, Epistle 12 to Olympiada.

7 Nicephorus Theotokos, Archbishop of Astrakhan, Homily for the Second Sunday of Great Lent.

8 Optiniskii Starets Hilarion, (Platina, CA 1979), p. 216.

9 St. Isaac of Syria, *Ascetic Homilies*, Boston MA 1984, p. 289.

10 St. John Chrysostom, Commentary on the Gospel of St. John, homily 85 #2.

11 St. John of Kronstadt, *My Life in Christ* (Jordansville, NY 1984), p. 404.

References

Eppinger, Josh (1991). The invasion of the ethicists. *Medical Tribune*, May 2, p. 10.

Gillon, Raanon (1990). Death. *Journal of Medical Ethics*, no. 16, p. 4.

Harakas, S. (1980). *For the Health of the Body and Soul.* Brookline, Massachusetts: Holy Cross Orthodox Press, p. 35.

Kriegle, D. (1991). Unpublished letter to John Johnstone, March 8, p. 3.

La Puma, John, Orentlicher, David, and Moss, Robert J. (1991). Advance directives on admission. *Jama*, July 17, vol. 266, no. 3, p. 403.

Rix, B.A. (1990). Danish ethics council rejects brain death as the criterion of death. *Journal of Medical Ethics*, no. 16, p. 6.

White, Margot L., and Fletcher, John C. (1991). The patient self determination act. *Jama,* July 17, vol. 266, no. 3, pp. 410-12.

Wisdom of Jesus, Son of Sirach 7:36.

PART IV

Genetic and Bio-Engineering

Nowhere are the creative aspects of modern science and modern man more dramatic and evident than through recent efforts that have unveiled the secrets of life itself (genetic engineering) and recreating organs and body parts (bio-engineering). The enthusiasm for extending and improving life through such measures has also resulted in a legal frenzy to protect human rights. This torrent of activity has required ethical and religious direction to calm the potentially explosive issues inherent in the new technologies.

Dr. Demetrios Demopulous explains the role of molecular genetics in his discussion of "Ethics and Genetic Engineering." He provides the basis needed for directing the ethical issues of science with his understanding of Orthodox anthropology.

Dr. Frank Papatheofanis provides a history of organ transplantations followed by an examination of Orthodox Scripture and Tradition that provide direction for addressing concerns about organ transplantation.

Dr. Sharon Chirban explains the psychological and spiritual consequences of organ transplantation based upon a wholistic concept of self/soul from the Orthodox Christian tradition. She offers the image of the body as both "self" and "sacred" as required in moral decision making concerning organ transplantation.

Ethics and Genetic Engineering

Demetrios Demopulos

Molecular genetics is the branch of biology that investigates the molecular structure and behavior of the genetic material, the nucleic acids which encode, transcribe, and translate primary protein structure. The determinant for primary protein structure is the gene, a stretch of necleotides residing at a certain position along the DNA chain that comprises the heart of the chromosome. The molecular geneticist is interested in learning the structure of the gene, that is, the nucleotide sequence; the organization of the chromosome in the vicinity of the gene; and the interactions of the gene with various proteins that regulate its expression. Methodologies developed to study these problems provide the tools for genetic engineering. These basic tools are *restriction fragment length analysis and nucleotide sequencing.*

Restriction fragment length analysis relies on microbial restriction enzymes which selectively cut DNA at a specific recognition sequence, usually four or six nucleotides long. If a sufficiently large DNA molecule is treated with a restriction enzyme, it will be cleaved into discrete fragments whose length depends on the position of restriction sites in the DNA. These fragments can then be separated by electrophoresis through a porous support medium, such as an agarose gel, resulting in a distinct ladder of fragments. Treatment of another molecule with the same enzyme often results in a different pattern of fragments, as random mutation will eliminate some restriction sites and create others. The use of an appropriate probe allows comparisons to be made between individuals on the basis of these restriction fragment patterns. This is the basis for DNA fingerprinting, the latest forensic technique, as well as for most molecular gentic screens for genetic disorders.

Nucleotide sequencing employs the DNA replication enzymes of a bacteria with chemically altered nucleotides. Using a specific DNA fragment as a template, one can synthesize a complementary replica through the action of the bacterial enzyme. If a small proportion of a chemically altered nucleotide is added to normal nucleotides, DNA synthesis will stop wherever an altered nucleotide is attached. Because of the small number of altered nucleotides, the termination will occur at random. For example, if the sequence of a DNA fragment is:

AGTCCGATACAT

and an altered C is included in the reaction, the following fragments will be synthesized:

AGTC, AGTCC, AGTCCGATAC, and AGTCCGATACAT

If parallel synthesis reactions are conducted on the same DNA template, with each reaction containing a different altered nucleotide, and the products are separated by electrophoresis, the sequence of the template can be read.

Restriction fragment length analysis allows one to isolate a segment of DNA, and sequence analysis allows one to determine its primary structure. Modification of these basic techniques allows us to synthesize genes and to transfer them to other cells. The latter ability interests us here. Restriction fragments can be spliced into plasmides (naturally occurring, circular extrachromosomal DNA molecules found in bacteria and yeast) which can be put back into bacteria or yeast in order to "grow" large quantities of the fragment of large quantities of the gene product. This is the basic method by which human insulin is produced. The insulin gene is put into a microorganism, which then produces insulin from the human template.

Alternatively, the gene of interest can be put into mammalian cells, in vitro, to study gene expression. I was involved in a study of aplolipoprotein Al regulation where I routinely studied the transient expression of a rat gene in human liver cells.

Finally, the gene of interest can be introduced and incorporated into the genome of a cell or cell line thereby altering the genotype of the cell-- altering what the cell makes or what it looks like. This is the area of genetic engineering.

Molecular screening and genetic engineering have been employed in both plant and animal breeding. From the trivial, albeit lucrative engineering of a white-petaled chrysanthemum, to the introduction of pest and disease resistance genes into food crops, molecular genetics is contributing to plant breeding. This story is repeated in animal research, from the introduction of a gene encoding rat growth hormone into the mouse, creating a "supermouse" (basically to see if it would work), to the transfer of desirable genes into cattle. Cattle are also being cloned, that is, embryos are disassociated and each pluripotent cell is allowed to develop into an animal, thus creating gentically identical clones by the same process that monozygotic twins occur naturally. I should add, here, that genetic engineering has been practiced since plants and animals were domesticated. The only difference is that before the new technology, the breeder had to wait for natural genetic changes from which to select the desired trait.

This discussion so far has been a brief background to the main issue of the use of molecular genetics in medicine. I will now attempt to describe the current use of molecular genetics in screening for genetic disorders and to project some possible uses for genetic engineering in gene therapy.

The underlying basis of my discussion is grounded in what I hope is an Orthodox understanding of anthropology. The human being was created in the image of Christ, Who is the image of God. Therefore, humanity is the "image of the Image" (Nellas, p. 24).

Human ontology, therefore, is iconic. Human nature in this sense is a process of moving toward the Archtype which is Christ incarnate. Seen as a process, human nature is not realized until humanity achieves hypostatic union with God. Humanity "finds in the Archetype [its] true ontological meaning" (Nellas, p.37).

Another aspect of humanity is its link between God and the rest of the created world-- humanity as microcosm and mediator. According to St. Maximos:

> Man was introduced . . . as a natural bond mediating between the extremes of the whole through his own parts, and bringing into unity in his own person those things which by nature are far distant from each

his own person those things which by nature are far distant from each
other (St. Maximos).

As such, humanity is a microcosm, containing all the distinctions of
the created world (Thunberg, 1985).

The purpose of humanity in this sense, then, is two-fold, to proceed
toward union with God and achieve ontological actualization, and to
bring the rest of creation with it. In its natural state, humanity and all
of creation were harmoniously moving towards transfiguration. The
fall, however, changed all of that. When humanity turned away from
its purpose and goal, it lapsed into an unnatural state. As the link
between God and creation, it carried the rest of nature with it. Natural
laws continued to function but in a disorderly fashion. Creation was
placed in a state of "constant flux, mutation, and change" (Nellas, p.
48).

It is in this unnatural, lapsed nature that we find ourselves today.
We find ourselves in a world full of disease and genetic disorders.
We also have developed technologies to study and treat these
disorders. Nellas finds in the writings of St. John Chrysostom that

The saints . . . rejoice and glorify God for the new technical skills with
which men in the midst of the new needs of every exercise stewardship over
their world (Nellas, p. 98).

Now, it seems to me that each human being should be given as
great an opportunity as possible to achieve ontological actualization,
union with God. One way to allow this is to help people live as long
as possible, "to aid others in reducing the evil of sickness in this life"
(Harakas). I think that molecular genetics and genetic engineering
can play a valuable role in achieving these goals.

Molecular Genetic Screening
    Screening on the molecular level usually employs restriction
fragment length analysis using enzymes and probes that differentiate
between the normal and the defective gene, or that differentiate
markers that are tightly linked to the locus of this disease. In adults
and children, the source of DNA is usually peripheral leucocytes,
while prenatal screening uses cells obtained from the amniotic fluid,
or by sampling the chorionic villus. Conditions that can be screened
for include thalassemias, sickle cell anemia, cystic fibrosis, al

antitrypsin deficiency, phenylketonuria, Duchennes and Becker muscular dystrophy and Huntington's chorea.

Beta-thalassemias are common genetic disorders among Mediterranean peoples. The frequency of defective beta-globin genes is relatively high in these populations because the heterozygous condition-- one normal allele and one defective allele-- allowed resistance to malaria. The homozygous condition-- two defective alleles-- results in the lethal thalassemia major condition.

Screening for defective beta-globin gene in these populations could identify carrieres among adults. Once identified, they would be informed of the risk of having an affected child. If, however, both are carriers, the probability of having an affected child is one in four. These couples could then be counselled for appropriate child bearing choices. They may opt for not having children, or for "taking their chances." They could also opt for fetal screening. If screening indicates an affected fetus, the parents could choose to have an abortion or could better prepare themselves for caring for a thalassemic child.

Is genetic screening ethical in this case? I would answer yes. People should be given access to information to allow them to better plan their families. The choices they make may or may not be ethical, and it is the responsibility of genetic counselors and those who minister to these people to help them make the right choice.

Another example of the use of genetic screening is more difficult to evaluate. Huntington's chorea is caused by a dominant mutation and results inneurological degeneration and death. Afflicted people usually do not show symptoms until their 40's, long after most people have begun families. Because it is inherited in a dominant manner, one-half of the offspring of an affected individual are expected to be afflicted.

Currently there is no treatment or cure for this disorder. There is, however, a molecular marker that can be used to screen for the presence of the defective gene. The screening protocol and determination of affliction is more complex than the case of thalassemia and will not be discussed here.

I would like to consider the ramifications of screening for this disease. In the case of thalassemias, healthy adults were informed of the risk of bearing afflicted children. In this case, healthy adults are informed of the possible manner of their own demise. Should the screen be offered? If yes, should it be offered indiscriminately--

should it be offered to anyone who requests it? Can members of a family with a history of Huntington's chorea be forced to submit to the screen? These are difficult questions. It seems clear to me that members of an affected family should be tested if that is their choice. However, counselling is extremely important to help positives cope with their fate. I would argue, as do geneticists involved in developing and applying the test, that intensive counselling be given *before* an individual is tested. This would help people decide if they really want to be tested and help them cope with the results.

In this case, as in many cases of screens for genetic disorder, the ability to detect is far ahead of the ability to treat. This reality makes it difficult to decide what is the right thing to do. The research that leads to a screen for a genetic disorder may, however, subsequently provide the treatment.

Gene Therapy

Genetically engineered lymphocytes are currently in clinical trials as treatment for some inoperable cancers. It is only a matter of time until the technology is available actually to treat simple genetic disorders with gene therapy. Research is progressing on ways to introduce functional genes into the appropriate cells to correct genetic deficiencies. Research is also underway to turn off genetically genes whose expression cause disease.

There is probably nothing more controversial in modern genetics than the specter of genetically engineered humans. Many of the negative images concern the cloning of humans-- making replicas of a desired genotype as in Huxley's *Brave New World* or the concerns of Ramsey and others. Other concerns are molecular eugenics, the ability to introduce desirable traits into the human germ line. The immediate use of genetic engineering, however, will be the correction, in somatic tissue, of genetic defects. This will not be without ethical considerations. By way of example, I will propose a hypothetical, albeit realistic, situations that may be faced in the near future.

Cystic fibrosis is a recessive genetic disorder that affects mucous secretions and leads to fatal lung disease and pancreatic dysfunction. Afflicted individuals usually die in their teens. Thus, the disorder is for all practical purposes, "genetically lethal."

The population genetics of recessive lethals tells us that the frequency of the deleterious allele will decline over generations as the homozygotes will be unable to contribute to the gene pool. Given the occurrence of cystic fibrosis as 1 in 1000, the frequency of the deleterious allele is 0.032. A simple calculation of the change in gene frequency, without taking into account the mutation rate to a deleterious form, reveals that after 10 generations the gene frequency will have been reduced to 0.022, or 1 afflicted individual in 2000. If homozygotes could reproduce normally, the gene frequency would tend to remain at 0.032, and the incidence of affected people would remain at 1 in 1000. Actually, the frequency would tend to increase due to mutation, but at a slight, almost negligible rate. Even if the frequency of incidence remains the same, the absolute number of affected individuals will increase as the number of people increases. With this background, let us consider the situation.

Suppose that, though modern biotechnology, we are able to cure victims of cystic fibrosis by gene therapy. These people, who would normally die in their teens, could then lead normal, productive, and reproductive lives. They would pass on the deleterious genes to their offspring. Suppose, also, that this therapy is expensive, and drains the resources of an already fiscally compromised public health system. As more people are born with cystic fibrosis, greater resources will be required to cure them, further depleting public health funds. What, then, are we to do?

Taking a utilitarian approach to the problem, we find that to provide a cure to all who need it may be ethical if it provides the greater good to the most people. Alternatively, exhausting funds for a minority of individuals may be deemed harmful to most people, and so gene therapy may be considered unethical.

As Orthodox Christians, we must approach the problem as one of dealing with a person created in the image and likeness of God. As such, this person must have every opportunity to grow and develop spiritually to reach ontological actualization. If gene therapy can assist in prolonging life productively, it should be allowed. One can counter with the argument that more people will have the possibility of theosis if gene therapy is not allowed, because funds will be available for common medical treatment, etc. I think we must reject this argument. If we have a treatment for the symptoms of a disease, we must use it to alleviate suffering, to allow each person every opportunity to grow spiritually.

We already have examples of the use of new treatments to alleviate disease. Besides the obvious immunization requirements to combat communicable diseases such as polio and measles, there is a standard neonatal test for phenylketonuria, a genetic disorder which leads to severe, mental retardation if left untreated. In this case, treatment is effected through controlled diet, restricting the intake of phenylalanine. Also diabetics routinely take insulin, without which they would quickly die. I do not think anyone would question the ethics of using these treatments.

The treatment of phenylketonuria is simple and inexpensive. Treatment of other disorders by gene therapy may not be so. The question is, then, what do we do with people who survive genetic lethal conditions? Do we limit reproductive rights of genetically treated individuals?

The simple answer is no. We cannot proscribe people from reproducing short of forced sterilization, and I do not believe that is an ethical alternative. We can, however, attempt to educate those people as to the consequences of reproduction. When properly informed, they may wish to have their own children, or they may wish to adopt some of the many parentless children who exist in this country and the world. Adult screening would allow couples to determine the probability of conceiving an afflicted child.

Another solution to this dilemma is to apply genetic engineering to the germ line, to replace the defective gene, or add a functional gene that would effectively cure the problem. This is absolutely unethical.

For technical reasons, introducing a functional gene into a genome could result in further deleterious effects due to disruption of genetic material upon insertion. This problem could be solved be replacing the defective gene with a functional copy through recombination. This is being researched in mice. However, the methodology by which a functional gene could replace a defective gene requires in vitro manipulation of embryos and selection for successful incorporation. The unaltered embryos would then be discarded. Our belief in the sanctity of human life at any stage of development forbids us to consider this a reasonable or ethical alternative.

We also just do not know enough about gene interactions and pleiotrophic effects to ensure that we are not causing more serious damage for future generations. As discussed above, heterozygotes for thalassemia are resistant to malaria, and that is why the incidence of thalassemia is so high. As for our dilemma, no known advantage is gained by heterozygosity for the cystic fibrosis gene. However, its relatively high frequency suggests that there is an advantage. We do not know that if we correct the lethal gene, we would not be creating a similarly devastating condition.

Our gene pool is the result of tens of thousands of years of natural selection, millions of years of selection if we consider our progenitor species. There are conditions that cause us pain and misery, but I believe that God has His hand in evolution. He created us through evolution, and our current biological condition is his gift to us to allow us to achieve our potential-- to become united with Him. He has also given us the ability to fix our bodies when they break down, and we must use that gift wisely. Only God knows the consequences of altering the human germ line. It is not for us to attempt to manipulate our future generations.

References

Harakas, S. (1980). *For the Health of the Body and Soul*. Brookline,
Massachusetts: Holy Cross Orthodox Press, p. 42.

Nellas, Panayiotis (1987). *Deification In Christ, The Nature of the Human Person*. Crestwood, NY: St. Vladimir's Seminary Press.

St. Maximos the Confessor, *Ambigua* 41, in Nellas, op. cit. p. 212.

Thunberg, L. (1985). *Man and the Cosmos, The Vision of St. Maximus the Confessor*. Crestwood, NY: St. Vladimir's Seminary Press.

An Orthodox Christian Perspective on Organ Transplant

Frank J. Papatheofanis

The frontiers of science are vast and surprisingly limitless. As human beings, our passion for discovery and invention has driven us at a feverish pace while our ability to appreciate the consequences of such scientific discoveries on our civilization has lagged behind. Remarkable technological successes in the biomedical sciences, in particular, have provided science watchers and consumers with marvelous treats from the laboratory. Moreover, our epoch has been heralded as the age of molecular medicine because of the fresh understanding gained from studying the human genome. Recent discoveries in chromosomal mapping have identified defective genes involved in cystic fibrosis, Alzheimer's disease, and colon cancer. These impressive discoveries resulted from a concerted scientific effort to map and to understand the machinery of the human genome for the purpose of understanding human biology and improving human health.

Not to be outdone by the successes of the life sciences, innovations in the engineering and physical sciences have also resulted in a markedly improved understanding of disease and the creation of additional options for the modern armamentarium poised to combat human suffering and death. A new artificial heart, the Jarvik 2000, is currently being tested at the Texas Heart Institute. Artificial organs from the lungs to the pancreas to blood and blood products are still in development whereas artificial hips and knees are commonplace. The combined efforts of the life and physical sciences have resulted in discoveries that relieve human suffering, prolong and improve life, and save the local and national economies billions of dollars each year. These discoveries have surpassed any expectations formulated only a decade or two ago, and the scientific enterprise promises to continue delivering more useful information in the future.

Many medical discoveries have captured the attention of our 20th century civilization, unlike any previous century in history. For example, the discovery of insulin by Banting and Best in 1922 represented a singular achievement in our understanding of physiology. It also served as a singular achievement in the lives of millions of diabetics who would have died had this discovery not been made. Before insulin, diabetics endured a slow death characterized by progressive physical wasting and mental deterioration.

Another singular discovery was marked by Fleming's introduction of penicillin in 1941 that resulted in the saving of countless lives that would otherwise have succumbed to infection. Penicillin ushered in the antibiotic era that continues to evolve to this day since antibiotics remain a cornerstone in the treatment of infection. A third major discovery of this century with far-reaching and long-term significance was the introduction of extracorporeal hemodialysis by Scribner in 1960. Patients in renal failure died as a result of the toxins that accumulated in their circulation. Hemodialysis represented a method for cleaning that blood supply and restoring life to an otherwise doomed patient.

Other noteworthy discoveries were made during this century but those above have been highlighted for a reason. At the time of their introduction to the world community, all of those discoveries were used on an extremely limited scale because of their short supply. Insulin was administered to wealthy, well-connected patients who could afford it, penicillin went to combat soldiers during World War II, and hemodialysis was made available to carefully selected patients who endured a complex lottery selection system and rigorous review by bioethics committees. The laboratories offered these life-saving measures objectively and without pre-determined allocation agendas but their scarcity required careful rationing and control.

Soon after these discoveries were introduced, tremendous effort went into increasing their production and availability to the point where all of these resources became generally available. These discoveries forced our society, at different junctures, to consider the difficult issue of allocation of extremely limited, life-sustaining resources. In each case, the increased availability of the resources themselves eventually undermined and rendered unnecessary the decisions and decision-making process regarding their allocation. In other words, as more hemodialysis units were built and used, ethics committees no longer faced the dilemma of choosing patients to undergo the intervention. Unfortunately, this has not been the case with each medical discovery born out of the investigational efforts of this century.

In this regard, the most dramatic example of the conflicts arising from the ethical allocation of life-giving measures that applies to the general population involves the transplantation and replacement of the human heart. This story serves as a model for discussing the ethical distribution of scarce human organs. The transplantation of the human kidney, liver, or lung serves as an alternative model, and debates are currently underway in the determination of the ethical distribution of these other organ systems. The development of the successful cardiac transplantation required considerable experimental investigation involving modification of existing surgical techniques, the design and construction of precise physiological monitoring and regulation, instrumentation, and immunological modification.

Early experimental work started at the turn of the century, and Alexis Carrel performed the first experimental transplant in 1905. Carrel was widely recognized for his work and received the Nobel Prize in 1912 for his pioneering investigations on the circulation and anastomosis of blood vessels. V. B. Demikhov in Russia, furthered his work during the 1930's through the 1950's. Not until 1961, however, under Norman Shumway's leadership, did the first successful transplantation of a living heart from one living animal to another occur. Three years later, James Hardy transplanted a chimpanzee's heart to a human recipient, and, in 1967, Christian Barnard performed the first successful human-to-human heart transplantation.

The addition of the immunosupressive agent cyclosporine in 1976 reduced the initial rejection by body organs. Heart transplants have

now become ordinary in the medical community with some 3000
performed annually, (Figure 4.1)

Figure 4.1 Heart Transplants Worldwide

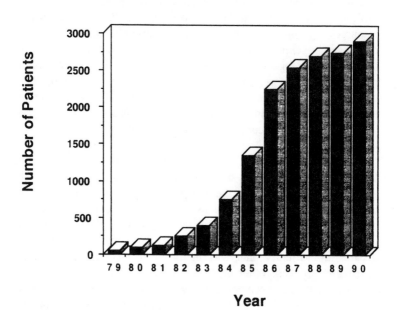

and over 80% of recipients survive for at least five years. They have
become an accepted treatment option in cardiovascular therapy and
received approval for Medicare funding. Transplantation of lungs and
heart-lung systems remains technically more difficult. They
physiological derangements that follow such transplantation
procedures are far more complex than those involving heart
transplantation.

To perform a heart transplantation, a donor heart is needed. No
amount of technical wizardry can circumvent this obvious
requirement. Artificial hearts are in various stages of development
but their availability and usefulness remains a distant hope at this
point.   At best, some have argued for their use as "bridges" in
sustaining a recipient while a donor is identified. As a result, our
society is again faced with limited resources in dealing with the needs
of recipients.   This shortage of donor hearts creates an ethical
dilemma in that an equitable allocation system must be created for the

distribution of available hearts. This dilemma has been in place for almost 20 years, and it remains a treacherous topic for institutional ethics committees, physicians, and, most importantly, individual patients and their families.

To address some of the dilemmas or issues involving the transplantation of human organs, as Orthodox Christians, we turn to Scripture and Holy Tradition. As Orthodox, the issue of organ transplantation itself does not offer any direct challenge to Scripture or Tradition. The body, or σῶμα, is mentioned in the Scriptures over thirty times. Without attempting an exegesis of the uses and meanings of this word, we have come to understand the *body* as representing a variety of meanings including Christ's Church ["and He has put all things under His feet and has made Him the head over all things for the church, which is His body, the fullness of Him who fills all in all," (Ephesians 1: 22-23, RSV)], the members of His church ["Do you not know that your bodies are members of Christ?" (Corinthians 6: 15, RSV)], and the temple of the Holy Spirit ["Do you not know that your body is a temple of the Holy Spirit within you, which you have form God? You are not your own: you were bought with a price. So glorify God in your body" (Corinthians 6: 19-20, RSV)].

Clearly, our body is not our own-- it belongs to God. Our mortal existence is incomplete and we can only achieve wholeness and completeness when we are with God in heaven ["Without having seen Him you love Him; though you do not see Him you believe in Him and rejoice with unutterable and exalted joy. As the outcome of your faith you obtain the salvation of your souls." (Peter 1: 8-9, RSV)]. As a result, our bodies, and the organ systems that comprise them, belong to God for His purposes. Holy Tradition amplifies this attitude towards our bodies in the often told story of one of the miracles of Saints Cosmas and Damian, the Holy Unmercenaries, who were martyred in 303 A.D. (one of three sets of brothers who were physician-saints). One version of the miracle was recently retold by the noted medical historian and ethicist Albert R. Jonsen:

> Twin brothers from Asia Minor, Cosmas and Damian, practiced medicine without fee. They were martyred for their Christian faith and came to be venerated throughout Christendom as the patron saints of physicians. Legend credits them with the first transplantation surgery. The saintly physicians appeared in a vision to a man sleeping in the

church built in their honor in Rome. The man suffered from a gangrenous leg and had come to the Church to petition the saints to intercede. From heaven the brothers heard the man's prayer, and while he slept amputated the leg and replaced it with a "healthy" leg taken from a corpse. The patient was white, the donor was black (as was the case with one of the first heart transplants in South Africa). Presumably the sleeping recipient did not give "informed consent" nor did the cadaver have a signed donor card. The holy physicians saved the life of their patient and left him with a miscegenetic limb. The saints performed a miracle, for there was no natural way in which a limb from a corpse (unless he was brain dead but still on a respirator, which the story does not indicate) [sic] would thrive on their patient. But their miracle was marred and inept in several ways; while its efficacy derived from a divine source, its performance was by human skills. Presumably even saints can be clumsy. [sic] The work of the holy physicians suggests a good way to view the miracles of modern medicine: as wondrous in comparison with the alternatives, but ambiguously so (Johnson, 1990, pp. 136-137).

This illustration points towards an Orthodox stand on organ transplantation and sets the stage for discussing some indirect challenges offered by the issue of heart transplantation for all Christians.

Some key questions remain in the ethical allocation of human hearts. For example, who decides where the limited donor hearts are implanted? This is a pivotal question in the ethics of transplantation. Some specific, widely-used selection criteria are listed in Figure 4.2[1]:

Absolute	Relative
Active infection	Advanced age
Untreated malignancy	*Unresolved* pulmonary embolism
Co-existing systemic illness that may limit life expectancy	Insulin-requiring diabetes mellitus
Irreversible and severe dysfunction of any other major organ system (liver, lung, kidney)	Significant peripheral vascular or cerebrovascular disease
High fixed pulmonary vascular resistance	Drug addiction, alcoholism, mental illness or psychological instability

Figure 4.2

Likewise, specific criteria are employed in the selection of a suitable donor including donor age (up to 60 years), donor size (body mass within 25% of the potential recipient), donor blood group, exclusion of cardiovascular disease (e.g., hypertension, diabetes), and exclusion of transferable disease (e.g., malignancy or HIV). The major source of donor hearts remains the person who has died of head injury or spontaneous intracranial hemorrhage-- the brain dead donor. Other ethical considerations include authorization of donation and acquisition of hearts or other tissues-- who has the legal and moral authority to implement the removal and transfer of organs after death? Also, can such organs be sold in a legitimate commercial marketplace? Can corporations specializing in the procurement and sale of donor organs earn profits from their dealings?

By far, the most serious ethical question arises from the observation that hundreds of people die every day but a shortage of donor hearts persists for over 20 years since the widespread introduction of transplantation surgery. According to Gallup polls, 80% of Americans claim their willingness to donate their organs and tissues for transplantation after death. Only 17%, however, carry an organ donor card. Over thirty percent of medically approved cardiac transplantation recipients die while awaiting a donor. When families are asked to consider organ donation at the time of a relative's death, over 70% accede to some tissue donation. Failure to understand the procedure of organ donation and transplantation has led to the short supply of available hearts. Common concerns include: 1) a lack of awareness of religious or moral propriety of distortion of the body or removal of organs and tissues for transplantation, 2) fear of disrespect by caretakers for the corpse after organ donation, 3) concern that the organs will be sold or marketed, 4) a superstition that holds that talk of death or consenting to organ donation might hasten the demise of the donor, and 5) a concern that organs will be removed while the donor is still functionally alive (Davis, 1986).

Some of these concerns are difficult to dispel in the minds of many Americans. As Christians, however, these concerns should not bar us from organ donation. Distortion of the body is probably the most often cited reason some Christians give to avoid the issue of donation. They argue that the resurrection of the body promised in Scripture would produce a noticeable distortion of their earthly body if organs are missing. They point to the condemnation of cremation by the

Orthodox Church as further testimony that one should not tamper with
the body. These long-standing misunderstandings act to perpetuate
the unwillingness of many Orthodox Christians to consider organ
donation. Reason and knowledge of church history, however, readily
clarify these misunderstandings. For example, what could distort the
body more than decades or centuries of internment within the earth
after burial? Does the loss of one's useful heart add anything to this
total dissolution of the flesh? As for the issue of cremation, the
Church objects to this practice because it represents an 18th century
symbol of the rejection of Christianity that was practiced by the
rationalists of the "Enlightenment." It has nothing to do with potential
distortion of the body at the time of Judgment.

The Orthodox Church holds no official position on the issue of
organ transplantation-- it neither encourages nor condemns this
practice. The Church has existed for centuries without accounting for
every advancement in science or learning. But the changes brought
through scientific inquiry today are far more complex, and occurring
at such an accelerated rate, that the Church's teachings on these
questions would provide far-reaching guidance and timeliness. How,
then, can Orthodox Christians arrive at a meaningful understanding of
the significance of transplantation in view of Christian teaching and
Tradition?

First, we must turn to God through prayer, fasting, and
understanding of His Word in Scripture and Tradition. Second, we
must shed our cultural beliefs in a manner that respects those
traditions of thought and action but upholds only that which is
valuable to an emerging civilization trapped in an era of materialism
and polytheistic and mystical faith systems. Finally, we must
appreciate that the anatomical, physiological, and psychological forms
and functions that characterize the human being are inseparable from
health and disease in the context of a mortal world.

Our spiritual life is closely linked to our finite, mortal life. We
have been created in spirit, and *flesh*. Harakas argues that we
individually represent a "microcosm":

> Concurrently, the understanding of the human which sees it as a
> microcosm, unites humanity with the non-human material world. The
> human condition relates to the earthly aspects of created existence as
> well as to the Creator. As such, it directly influences our thinking about
> the integrity of creation. As is well known, Eastern Orthodoxy's view of

human nature is dynamic. Two other ways that are articulated is through the Patristic understanding of the creation of humanity in the image and likeness of God, and through the Chalcedonian doctrine of the Person of Jesus Christ. Both serve to give content to a vision of high human potential in spite of the reality of the fallen and distorted condition in which all of creation is found. Humanity as "microcosm" may serve equally as well to approach the subject (Harakas, 1988, p. 29).

Harakas continues, discussing the teachings of St. Gregory of Nazianzus,

In this understanding of human existence there is a perception of a deep connectedness with the material side of created reality. St. Gregory says that we are fully involved in the material creation by nature of our physical existence, and implied is the opposite, i.e., that the material created reality is deeply involved with us. Should we move in the direction of deification of our nature in progress toward God, we will somehow carry the created material world with us. Should we move in the opposite direction, the created material world will suffer with us as well (Harakas, 1988, pp. 30-31).

Our spiritual and material creation serves a Divine Purpose. This Creation, this "microcosm," that each human being represents and embodies is one of God's gifts to humanity, His Creation. As previously stated, neither our *bodies*, nor our souls for that matter, belong to us but to our Creator. We were created to serve God [His master said to him, "Well done, good and faithful servant; you have been faithful over a little, I will set you over much; enter into the joy of your Master" (Matthew 23:11, RSV)]. Does not the loving act of donating our heart or kidney or liver at the time of death represent love and service to our fellow man and Lord? How can such an act of giving be interpreted in any other way?

Our understanding of the need to give of our *body* in such a manner must also account for our understanding of the importance of this *body* and the maintenance of good health. We turn to St Diadochos who writes to his brethren monastics in the *Philokalia*,

There is nothing to prevent us from calling a doctor when we are ill. Since Providence has implanted remedies in nature, it has been possible for human experimentation to develop the art of medicine. All the same we should not place our hope of healing in doctors, but in our true Savior and Physician, Jesus Christ (Rudder, p. 524).

We must also come to understand that a Holy Tradition of healing the body also originated in the Church. This tradition began with Jesus Christ and the countless miracles he performed ["And he went about all Galilee teaching in their synagogues and preaching the gospel of the kingdom and healing every disease and every infirmity among the people." (Matthew 4:23, RSV)]. This Tradition extended to the Byzantines who created the modern hospital and cared for the sick physically and spiritually, and whose physicians were also ordained priests (Miller, 1985). Finally, this Tradition continues today, and the many medical discoveries made by modern physicians and scientists are ultimately God's gifts to His Creation:

> Medicines and the skill of physicians are blessings from God. It is not *eo ipso* wrong for a Christian to employ them, but it is sinful to put one's faith in them entirely since, when they are effective, it is only because their efficacy comes from God who can heal without them. Thus to resort to physicians without first placing one's trust in God is both foolish and sinful. Likewise to reject medicine and the medical arts entirely is not only not recommended but is disparaged (Amundsen, 1982).

Organ transplantation, genetic engineering, antibiotics, hemodialysis, insulin, and the scores of other medical discoveries we have witnessed this century are, indeed, blessings from God. This recognition of the linkage between our mortal creation and our spiritual existence, and the appropriate treatment of the derangements that may occur to our physical health, provides a resounding affirmative response to Reverend John Breck's challenge, in biomedical technology of the Kingdom or of the cosmos? (*St. Vladimir's Theological. Quarterly,* 32:5, 1988). Biomedical technology, organ transplantation, and other medical advances are blessings from God and they are, most certainly, of His Kingdom. This realization sets the stage for an Orthodox perspective on organ transplantation.

Our discussion of organ transplantation has included a review of the ethical issues and general considerations faced in cardiac transplantation. Since an artificial heart has yet to provide an effective treatment for patients with irreversible, fatal heart disease, these patients continue to require donor hearts for their survival. So too, other patients with irreversible disease require donor livers or kidneys or other tissues. Donor hearts are primarily obtained from brain-dead donors. As Orthodox Christians, we have resisted lending full acceptance to the practice of organ donation that has been made possible through technological innovations. Yet the basis for our reservations does not appear to be rooted in Holy Scripture or Tradition. Instead, our misconception of the act of organ donation and transplantation blurs our ability to understand the loving significance of this act in the context of our Creation. If motivated by love for our fellow human being, the act of organ donation does not detract in any measure from our fullness as Christ's body. This decision should be explored individually through prayer and discussions with other faithful Christians. As a Church, we must responsibly present organ transplantation as an option that merits significant contribution to the life of another human being and as an option that merits significant contribution to the life of another human being, and as an option that is pleasing and glorifying to our Lord.

Acknowledgement

I am grateful to my wife, Dr. Julie A. Papatheofanis, for her helpful comments and support during the course of preparing this manuscript.

Notes

1 Adapted from DKC Cooper and D. Novitsky, *The Transplantation and Replacement of Thoracic Organs*, Kluwer Academic, 1990.

References

Amundsen, Darrel W (1982). Medicine and faith in the early Christianity. *Bulletin of Historical Medicine* 56:341.

Cooper, DKC and Navitsky, D. (1990). *The Transplantation and Replacement of Thorasic Organs*, Kluwer Academic.

Davis, F.D. *et al.*, (1986). Organization of an organ donation network. *Surgical Clinics of North America,* Volume 66, pp. 641-652.

Harakas, Stanley S. (1988). The integrity of creation and ethics. *St. Vladimir's Theological Quarterly.* Volume 32, p. 29.

Jonsen, Albert R. (1990). *The New Medicine and the Old Ethics.* Cambridge, Massachusetts: Harvard University Press.

Miller, Timothy S. (1985). *The Birth of the Hospital in the Byzantine Empire*, John Hopkins University Press.

Psychological and Spiritual Perspectives on Organ Donation

Sharon Chirban

Introduction

The last ten years has seen a growing number of organ transplants to sustain life for those suffering from kidney, heart, lung or liver failure. The immunosupressive drug cyclosporin has made organ transplanting a viable procedure because it prevents the rejection of transplanted organs while allowing the body to fight infection. However, due to the rapid growth of diversified uses for body parts, more people are wanting organs than are available. The Uniform Anatomical Gift Act and the 1984 National Organ Transplant Act limiting property rights to human tissue, have been adopted by all fifty states. People now have a "modified" property right to their organs; they cannot sell their organs, but they retain the right to donate them, and nobody has the right to take them away. The current supply system of organs, which relies heavily on cadavers, is believed to have many inherent limitations. It is proposed that one way to enhance the system is to develop a market for human body parts. The proposed market system assumes that a sufficient number of individuals would be motivated by financial rewards to offer their organs and subsequently increase the overall supply.

Those who favor markets in body parts do so primarily to increase efficiency. Those who oppose markets do so primarily on ethical grounds that markets will lead inevitably to the "commodification" of human beings and to severe abuses of human rights. Titmuss (1971) outlined in his book *The Gift Relationship: From Blood to Social Policy* a fierce debate over whether there should be markets in blood. He expressed the belief that blood is the lifeline that runs in the veins of every member of the human race, proving that the family of man is a reality. He expressed the concern that "commercialization of blood and donor relationships represses the expression of altruism, erodes the sense of community." He feared that organ markets would redistribute organs from the poor to the rich and generally lower ethical standards. Theologians, psychologists and philosophers have also voiced their objections to the idea of selling human organs.

They share the premise that an "organ market" is dehumanizing. They propose that a system based on economics and efficiency treats a human being as a means to an end rather than an end in itself. In this paper I draw out possible psychological and spiritual consequences of organ donation and transplantation on the human psyche and the human soul. A fundamental underlying assumption of my perspective is that the body and self/soul are intricately related. Proponents of the market system encourage that the body and self/soul be treated as independent entities. I support my position with psychological evidence and Orthodox theological doctrine which argue for the interdependence of body and self/soul. To demonstrate the impact of the relationship between body and self/soul on modern science and technology, several metaphors are discussed as organizing concepts.

Metaphors of the Human Body

To outline how perceptions of the body influence organ donation and transplantation, Belk (1990) notes that there are four common metaphors used to describe whether our bodies *are* us or whether they are *possessed* by us. The body has been regarded as a *machine*, as a particular type of possession or thing (a perspective dominant in 20th century medicine). Another metaphor is body as a *garden*, where the body is thought to be an object-- but a natural or organic object rather than a synthetic one (this metaphor has been easily extended to organ transplants as reflected in the terminology "harvesting and implanting organs"). The body as a *self* suggest that it is a central part of our identity and perception of ourselves. And the fourth metaphor, the body as a *sacred vessel* suggests that the body is a temple of God (Belk, 1990).

Belk (1990) notes that if the body is regarded as a machine or a garden, then the idea of interchangeable parts provides a compelling extension of these metaphors which are quite compatible with the idea of organ transplantation. In the metaphor, *the body as self*, the body is seen as a central part of who we are and integrally related with it. Organ donation, then, may be seen as a way to perpetuate the self but may present a problem to organ recipients who fear losing their "self" by joining with another. Often from a religious perspective the body has been considered a *sacred vessel*. The implication of this metaphor is that the mutilation of the body through the organ donation may be considered a sacrilege. The *body as self* and the *body as sacred* each present certain difficulties to soliciting and transplanting organs and are overlapping and mutually reinforcing (Belk, 1990).

My feeling is that *body as sacred* has the potential for moving into the dualistic split between body and soul. The structural emphasis on a *vessel* excludes the concept of a whole person with a dynamic spiritual identity, made of soul and body. It is on the two metaphors, *body as self* and *body as sacred* and *spiritual*, that emphasis will be placed in my attempt to present an integrated understanding of the psychological and spiritual impact of organ donation on the donor and recipient.

Human beings struggle with integrating a *psychological self*, identified with body parts, personality, familial and social relationships, with *spiritual self*, love of God and a search for holiness. It is with this integration in mind between body and psychological self and spiritual self that I will explore the impact of donating organs amongst human beings. I will first focus on the psychological dimension by working with the *body as self* metaphor.

Psychological Dimension

The psychological morbidity associated with organ transplantation has only recently been researched. One opinion asserts that "organ and tissue donation is perhaps the most severe and destructive assault the human psyche can receive" (Fellner & Schwartz, 1978). This perspective seems to reflect a profound belief in the *body as self*. It states that the physical disruption by donating and receiving an organ may have detrimental effects on psychological well-being. It should be made clear, however, that some patients seem to adjust fairly well, while others seem to need to work through a psychological integration, in which the organ from the donor is accepted physically as well as psychologically into a stable internal body image. The success of integration is said to be dependent on the *real*, as well as *fantasized* qualities of the *donor*, and *the relationship* (if any) *between the donor and the recipient* (Riether, 1990).

Michelle Kline (*Time*, 1991), a contestant in the 1989 Miss America pageant, who received a kidney from her brother, could not speak to him afterward, although they eventually reconciled. The gift weighed heavily on her: "It was a feeling of overwhelming debt that I could not repay." Another kidney donor became so depressed after the recipient did not thrive that he killed himself in despair. It is pretty well understood that his committing suicide is not completely explained by the rejection of the organ. It may be that the rejection of his organ produced an undurable psychic stress. In light of these kinds of incidents, the following suggestions have been made by Fox & Swazey (1977) when encouraging an organ donation:

1. Assess the meaning of the donation both to the donor and recipient;
2. Assess the implications for the personality integration and function of each of them, and;
3. Assess the extent to which the transplant might "bind" them one to the other or fuse their identities.

Psychological evidence generally suggests that our bodies are central to our identities. Research studies show that of all the tangible manifestations of the self, body and body parts are consistently found to be the most central to identity (Belk, 1987, 1988). There is a relative relationship between body, body parts, and identity. Not all people see their bodies as equally central to their identities and not all body parts are seen as equally central to the self. It has been proposed that the centrality of body organs to one's perception of self is related to *cathexis*, or the *emotional investment in one's body parts*. Visible body parts are central to perceptions of self because of the degree of control we exercise over them (Allport, 1937; McClelland, 1951). It was found that people who rated their general body image organs as less important to them are more willing to donate their body organs (Pessemier, Bemmaor, & Hanssens, 1977). Following this finding, the willingness to donate organs is understood as more of an act of *selflessness* (in the true sense of the word) beyond altruism, because those willing to donate organs had lower body investment scores than did those who were not willing to donate. Another factor in willingness to donate is that people are more willing to donate to those other persons seen as more central to their *selves*. It seems then that the emotional investment in specific others creates incentives for such donations. It may be that people choose to donate or not donate based on the importance of the "other" or the "body part" to the preservation of "self integration." The one more crucially important to self-integration is likely to be chosen.

There has been evidence, as suggested above that transplantation of important body organs can be psychologically traumatic. Both for donor and recipient there is the fear of *loss of self*. The trauma that generally results from organ transplantation involves a depression in the recipient that is at least partly due to psychological rather than physiological difficulties in accepting the new organ (Bernstein, 1977; Biorck & Magnusson, 1968; Klein & Simmons, 1977). The *body as self* is central to understanding the psychological dimensions involved in organ donation. It seems difficult to imagine a system which separates the body as a resupply vehicle without conceptualizing the emotional being attached to this vehicle. Now, I will turn to the metaphor of *body as sacred* and *spiritual*, and highlight some of the spiritual outcomes of organ transplantation, from an Orthodox perspective.

Spiritual Dimension

One religious perspective on the spiritual morbidity of transplanting organs can be extracted from Sherrard's (1987) statement that "the mechanistic character of modern science is marked by a desire to dominate, to master and to exploit nature, not to transform it or hallow it." Sherrard's perspective seems to be attacking the *machine* concept of modern medicine, which he suggests precludes the recognition of the *body as sacred*. Another religious perspective, however, might view donating organs as contributing to our sense of relationship and communion with others. This "life gift" can be understood as a real transcendence of the ego which is shared and passes on existence. The exclusiveness of the "self" is removed, and there is a shift and moving beyond our biological state of being. This perspective may be emphasizing the *body as spiritual* and *sacred* rather than just emphasizing the structural aspect of the body. By removing the "gift" in organ donation, the donor and recipient may be deprived of this opportunity to commune in this selfless and loving way. The result of "giftless" donating may be the exploitation of nature and incentive to control it, which may be what Sherrard's concern.

This difference in religious perspectives is explained by Zizioulas (1985) when describing the shift in relationship between science and theology:

> Science and theology for a long time seemed to be in search of different sorts of truth, as if there were not one truth in existence as a whole. This resulted from making truth subject to the dichotomy between the transcendent and the immanent, and in the final analysis from the fact that the "theological" truth and the "scientific" truth were both disconnected from the idea of communion, and were considered in terms of a subject-object framework which was simply the methodology of analytical research (p. 119-120).

A post-Einsteinian perspective suggests that it is possible to speak of a unique truth in the world, approachable scientifically and theologically. Therefore, this dualistic split is overcome through relationship, expressed in communion and self-transcendence. The theological perspective is also subject to this subject-object perspective and it seems important to keep the notion of communion in our religious understanding (e.g., of prostitution/sexual love). Orthodox theology of personhood tells us that the person represents not the relationship of a part to the whole, but the possibility of summing up the whole in a distinctiveness of relationship, through an act of self-transcendence (Zizioulas, 1985).

Orthodox Christianity also teaches that the whole person, body and soul was created for immortality. The doctrine of personhood, as body and soul, is clearly indicated in the prayers which are offered for the healing of the soul and body. Theologians agree that there is a bond of union between body and soul, with no conflict between them. The soul has a strong love for the body which does not want to separate from it (Papademetriou, 1989).

It is equally true that there is a close connection between body and soul in the act of donating or receiving an organ. Yannaras (1985) values the materiality of the body and is supportive of the Spirit-bearing potentialities of all material things (which in this case can be expressed in donating organs). Sherrard's perspective is consistent with that of Yannaras' in this way. Yannaras (1985) states that outside the communion of love the person loses their uniqueness and becomes a "thing" without an identity. Commodity-based perspectives like *machine* and *garden* (and possibly *sacred vessel*) threaten our perceptions of the body as a spiritual part of our selves. By retaining an organ distribution system which requires a "gift," a ritual is allowed that is social and spiritual rather than mechanistic. Orthodox theology has articulated the emptiness in the stance of an egoistic attitude in contrast to that of a dynamic identity when there is organic interdependence with the "other" (Florensky, 1914). It is the loving and self-sacrifice leading to interdependence, which facilitates an identity which is both psychologically sound and spiritually healthy. An orientation towards giving which leads to interdependence and wholeness, seems to be of interest for the developing soul and psyche.

Conclusion

It is evident that there are many complicating issues surrounding the donation of organs. The struggle between efficient distribution of organs through a market system and the current altruistic system, leaves open the discussion of the meaning and value of human life and human body parts. The contrasts displayed by the uses of different metaphors suggests a continuum of treating human beings as "things" or "spiritual entities." It seems necessary that Orthodox professionals who manage this issue from different disciplines (medical, psychological, and religious) develop an Orthodox perspective which attends to the many aspects of this dilemma which are often isolated and unintegrated. What is needed is a compassionate set of guidelines which helps to nurture those spiritually while struggling with the often painful limitations of our physical reality. A realistic struggle with the issue raised involves meeting individuals where they are and using such opportunities to help with providing care, support and healing rather than instituting a legalistic set of values. It is the task of Orthodox Christian professionals and clergy to find ways of managing Orthodox principles leading to "true" living with the sometimes harsh realities of our finite living.

References

Allport, G.W. (1937). *Personality: A Psychological Interpretation.* New York City, New York: Holt.

Belk, R.W. (1987). Possessions and the extended sense of self. In J. Umiker-Sebeok (Ed.), *Marketing and Semiotics: New Directions in the Study of Signs For Sale,* Berlin, West Germany: Mouton de Gryter, pp. 151-164. •

Belk, R.W. (1988). Possessions and the extended sense of self. *Journal of Consumer Research,* Issue 15, September, pp. 139-168.

Belk, R.W. (1990). Me and thee versus mine and thine: how perceptions of the body influence organ donation and transplantation. In Shanteau, J. & Harris, R. J. (Eds), *Organ Donations and Transplantation: Psychological and Behavioral Factors,* Washington, D.C.: APA.

Bernstein, D.M. (1977). Psychiatric assessment of the adjustment of transplanted children. In R.G. Simmons, S. Klein, & R. Simmons (Eds.), *Gift of Life: The Social and Psychological Impact of Organ Transplantation,* New York: Wiley, pp. 119-149.

Biorck, G., & Magnusson, G. (1968). The concept of self as experienced by patients with a transplanted kidney. *Acta Medica Scandinavia,* 183, pp. 191-192.

Fellner, C.H. & Schwartz, S.H. (1978). as cited in M.J. Saks, Social psychological contributions to a legislative subcommittee on organ and tissue transplants. *American Psychologist,* 33, p. 687.

Florensky, P. (1914). *The Pillar and Foundation of Truth-- An Essay in Orthodox Theodicy in Twelve Letters,* Moscow.

Fox, R.C. & Swazery, J.P. (1977). *The Courage to Fail: A Social View of Organ Transplants and Dialysis.* Chicago: University of Chicago Press.

Klein, S.D. & Simmons, R.G. (1977). The psychological impact of chronic kidney disease of children. In R.G. Simmons, S.D. Klein, & R.L. Simmons (Eds.), *Gift of Life: The Social and Psychological Impact of Organ Transplantation,* New York: Wiley, pp. 89-118.

McClelland, D.C. (1951). *Personality.* New York: Holt.

Papademetriou, G.C. (1989). The human body according to Saint Gregory Palamas. *Greek Orthodox Theological Review,* 34, no. 1, pp. 1-9.

Pessemeir, E.A., Bemmaor, A.C. & Hanssens, D.M. (1977). Willingness to supply human body parts: Some empirical results. *Journal of Consumer Research,* 47, January, pp. 131-140.

Time Magazine, (1991). Ethics: sparing parts. *Time,* 137, 24, pp. 54-58.

Titmus, R.M. (1970). *The Gift Relationship.* London: Allen & Unwin.

Yannaras, C. (1985). *The Freedom of Morality.* Crestwood, N.Y.: St. Vladimir's Seminary Press.

Zizioulas, J.D. (1985). *Being as Communion.* Crestwood, N.Y: St. Vladimir's Seminary Press.

PART V

Substance Abuse

Education about substances and their potential effects is an important aspect in the problem of drug misuse and abuse. By identifying the numerous biological, psychological, social and spiritual antecedents of substance abuse, the authors of this closing section provide insights about ethics and values that contribute to substance abuse.

In the opening article, "Drugs and the Family," discussion about the substance abuse is placed in the context of the family. Here the family's influences on human development and drug abuse is presented as "the spiritual antidote" for problems of substance abuse.

Lyn Breck confronts the topic of intervention, treatment and prevention of substance abuse in terms of the Church's role. She provides recommendations for a ministry to those afflicted with substance abuse as well as a call for honest assessment of how substance abuse prevails within the Church.

And, finally, James Campbell discusses the ethical issues of responsibility and repentance in view the problems of addiction and usury. By ascertaining the psychological, sociological, political, and theological aspects of substance abuse, Campbell argues that one needs to distinguish how different periods, changing values, and various psychological understandings affect the theology and ethics of both addiction and usury.

Drugs and the Family

John T. Chirban

Following the death of Elvis Presley, books and magazines exposed the gloomy inner world of the man heralded as the "King of Entertainment." In effect, Elvis was revealed as a self-taught pharmacologist who drugged himself to sleep with lethal doses of barbituates and cranked himself up with powerful stimulants; with the assistance of opportunistic doctors, dentists, and pharmacists. The toxicology report disclosed that Elvis consumed a litany of drugs 24 hours preceding his death: Codeine (at a concentration ten times higher than the toxic level), Morphine, Quaaludes, Valium, Diazepam Metabolite, Valmid, Placidytal, Amobarbital, Phenobarbitol, Carbital, Demoralan, and Phenylteloxamine. Drug abuse creates a destructive mind all its own. My comments are prepared not to address the more general crisis of drug abuse but actually to relate how particular values learned in the family may foster substance abuse, and how the family may provide a remedy to this problem.

By definition, drug abuse is a chemical issue. The antidote for drug abuse, however, is not medical or chemical, because the problem is often not drugs per se. Drug abuse is frequently a symptom of a disorder. *The Merck Manual*, the physician's guide to diseases, summarizes these origins of drug abuse: 1) pharmacologic factors and personality factors (Merck, 1982). But does this adequately explain drug abuse?

Etiology

The development of drug dependence is complex and unclear. The course of dependence is fueled by the addictive drugs themselves and by a predisposing condition, or the personality of the user. Addiction is partly related to cultural patterns and socioeconomic classes. Other factors involved in the mechanisms leading to drug abuse include group pressure, emotional distress, low self-esteem, social alienation, and environmental stress.

Two factors are, however, clearly indicated: pharmacology and personality. Pharmacologic factors show that persons who become addicted or dependent have no known biochemic predisposition to drugs, or psychological responsiveness, as compared to those who do not. The addictive personality has been described in various ways by behavioral scientists. Some have concluded that addicts are basically escapists who cannot confront reality. Addicts have also been described as schizoid individuals, fearful, withdrawn, and depressed with a history of frequent suicide attempts and self-inflicted injuries. Another opinion focuses on an addict's dependent nature, that they grasp in their relations and frequently exhibit overt and unconscious rage as well as immature sexuality (Merck, 1982). Nevertheless, there is little scientific evidence that characteristic personality factors exist.

Drug abuse painfully illustrates the story of the power of evil over life. The Greek word *diavolos*, or devil, actually, defines the course of drug abuse, as the word literally means "to divide." The signs of drug abuse are clearly divisions: dividing societies, families, one's self, and ultimately delivering the final division of life: death. The divisions caused by drug abuse paralyze our nation at all strata, from our heroes and leaders to our neighbors, and, most painfully, in our very homes. Drug abuse is a chemical, psychological, and spiritual collusion with *diavolia*, division. In order to plan an effective strategy to oppose and diffuse it, it is necessary to observe its course.

It may be most helpful to address the problems that lead to drugs. Successful antidotes for drug abuse are psychological and spiritual in nature. It is one's emotional life and spirituality gone awry that open the door to the twisted chemical highs and lows of drug abuse; healthy emotions and spirituality can reverse this situation.

The Family's Influence on Drug Abuse

A special issue of *Life* magazine portrays the devastation of our society by drug abuse. A mother observes that when she pulls out her pipe to smoke her drugs, her newborn baby begins to twist and resist. Sad, you say? "It makes me want to hit her," the mother responds. A 15-year-old crack addict works as a prostitute in exchange for drugs or cash to buy them. She charges $20 per customer, paying $5 an hour for use of a sofa, explaining, "Nobody likes to smoke alone." A son's love for his mother is expressed by buying crack for her. The article adds, however, that "he gets her drugs, but he has never kissed her" (Barnes, 1990). These individuals are the products of dysfunctional homes, lacking the sustenance of love and care. Their experience has not given rise to any positive emotions, so they hope the ingestions and injections of drugs will create those needed feelings.

Most scientists are not sure that they know why people use drugs in ways that are personally and socially destructive. We can categorize the theories explaining motivations into four major types. One group explains that "intrapsychic relationships," which create one's own mind or emotions are critical. A second focuses on "interpersonal relationships," interactions with others in social groups, and emphasizes psychological aspects as well as sociological influences. A third hypothesis postulates the impact of social structures, culture, and role expectation. A fourth explanation features biologically and physically based theories. While some theories focus on specific causative factors, others recognize the possibility of two or more factors interacting to account for drug abuse. I would like to add the spiritual factors to this classification of etiology.

My contention is that the environment of the drug abuser contributes to both the etiology and the cure of substance abuse. The range of addictions is wide and their causes are unclear. Some addictions to alcohol, for instance, may be caused, in part, by a person's genetic composition. But to the extent that we choose our addictions, we must look at this biological topic of drug abuse in terms of its social, psychological and spiritual aspects.

Clearly, our homes and learned attitudes seem to be significant factors in addiction. While most compulsive gamblers are men, most bulimics and anorexics are women. In effect, men have a fever to "make it big" by winning a fortune; women want to "make it small" through dieting. Men will say "It's a social thing," that all their friends go to bars, but women will talk about drinking in terms of altering feelings, to make them more sociable and less shy. We respond, in effect, to the roles proposed by culture and our environment. From this perspective, it is evident that our "nuclear environment," the family, greatly influences the behavior that we adopt.

Drug Abuse: A Family Affair

Increasing attention has been given by those who treat addictions to the importance of the family in origin, maintenance, and prevention of drug-related problems. Although experimental drug use by young people appears to be a social phenomenon, more serious drug use is predominantly a family problem. The changing nature of the family, including its mobility, changing traditions, instability due to divorce, and blending of families following remarriage, must be considered as we observe the growth of abuse.

Despite the many pro-drug influences of peers and the mass media, psychologists consider role modeling by parents the foremost factor in the development of young people's attitudes toward drugs and the likelihood that they will grow to abuse drugs. There appears to be a strong connection between parents' use of drugs and the incidence of drug use and abuse in their children. It is common knowledge that children of smokers tend to smoke themselves. If parents drink and take pills to escape personal problems, to feel better, or to have a good time, their children may grow up to believe that mood modification is the appropriate solution to disappointments and other forms of stress. This relationship between parental drug-taking behavior and that of their children is referred to as "modeling." An exception to this, however, can be in the case of adolescent's first use of legal alcohol, cigarettes, and illegal marijuana, which is mainly traceable to curiosity and heavy peer group influence. Research, however, demonstrates a striking relationship between parent-child interaction and the use of other illegal drugs.

A more subtle cause of drug abuse is family functioning. Family dynamics, including psychological forces and interactions, especially marked by poor communications, overinvolvement and overindulgence by parents, and punitive and psychologically distancing relationships between parents and children can provide a setting for a drug abuse problem.

In overt addiction, family members enable drug abuse to continue, whether unwittingly or intentionally, and the treatment of a chemically dependent individual is often delayed or sabotaged. In covert drug abuse the misbehavior of the addict "feeds" the peculiar psychological needs of other family members. Slowly, the drug user and the adverse consequences of drug abuse affects each member of the family. The non-abusers begin to display certain attitudes and behaviors in response to the disturbance. In an attempt to hide the problem, parents as well as siblings begin making excuses for the drug abuser's actions. Lying to protect the abuser serves to protect other family members from social embarrassment. In time, the entire family may rearrange daily routines to accommodate the abnormal drug use. Idle threats, blaming the drug abuser for all family problems, seeking revenge on the family destroyer, fears, feelings of shame, and even guilt are commonly experienced. Totally involved and endangered, the family is held captive by the drug abuser whose basic problem is still denied.

One of the issues frequently implicated in the subject of drug abuse is that of dependency. From a biological point of view, as social animals, we require dependency on others for survival. From a spiritual point of view, healthy dependency upon God is the only dependency we can count on! For those who are deaf to the faith, this idea cannot be heard. Traditional American values, moreover, foster independence to the exclusion of dependence. Yet healthy dependence is essential for the organism to survive and to prosper in relationships. But how does one learn healthy dependence and independence?

Dependency: A Spiritual Antidote

We are by nature dependent. The issue is, how have we learned to manage this human condition effectively? Or, to what degree do harmful encounters and experiences of dependency lead to the unhealthy dependency of drug abuse? We are social animals; denied such dependency, we become ill or die. Many people form at least part of their identity in terms of confused dependency. From a spiritual point of view, we meet our dependency needs through God, but what if we do not have Him? Where would we turn? Addiction is, in fact, often a condition of feeling deprived. It always exists within a special context of wanting more.

Research points out that children of addiction do not know how to leave home. We may move 10,000 miles away, but we take our homes with us, that is, the perspective and values taught by our family. Similarly, the parents of siblings with drug addiction may die, but without treatment, those affected never really get out. Homes where addiction was a problem drag this stone in their core into their jobs and relationships. Additionally, they drag in all the coping behaviors they have mastered in order to survive such families, even though many of these behaviors are now counterproductive. They impose these behaviors on their children, creating one of the great unrecognized "hangovers" of substance abuse-- children of abusers.

While other factors, environmental, physiological, economic, and genetic function critically in the origin of abuse, the family plays a dominant role in the genesis of drug problems. Our faith and family must teach us how the father of our childhood can be replaced by the God of adulthood; and the mother of childhood by the Mother Church. Healthy dependency on these archetypes can continue to nurture us. Unless one has been introduced to an applied faith to a cosistent spiritual practice in community, this does not occur. Such persons are divided from God the sustainer. The fruits of a healthy dependency are not maintained and these individuals seek dangerous alternatives.

From my clinical experience, I find that those who abuse drugs are often missing critical aspects of life: love, security, guidance, self-worth, trust, nurturing, the ability to express feelings, valuing one's own needs, and spontaneity. It is not by chance that I would also characterize a healthy Christian as having such traits. A vital spiritual experience provides the healthy Christian with these qualities. Furthermore, these must be the marks of functioning families as well as the larger functioning family that we call the Church. If there is an antidote to drug abuse, it is through making our families and Church functional and experiencing these qualities through our families. It is not by chance that dysfunctional families are devoid of these qualities and are unsuccessful in providing healthy, interdependent atmospheres. With only confusion about dependency, drug abusers seek security and feelings of self-worth in their addiction.

The Family and Primary Prevention

Although parents can engage effectively in secondary prevention by identifying chemical use in children and making appropriate interventions, the primary prevention of drug abuse demands a more positive and even more prolonged parental effort. Admittedly, no single method is guaranteed to prevent young people's involvement with drugs. However, there is considerable agreement that children who develop certain life skills or attributes within a healthy family will have little need of drug use, as they learn to manage their own lives effectively in a drug-using society. Characterized by the wholeness of each member, the healthy family is one that can develop in children clear ideas about themselves, others, and family boundaries, and the respect for differences as well as similarities. In this way, interdependency or independence is learned, and so is creating the critical balance of healthy lives, relationships, and marriages.

The Spiritual Problem

There is no question that in America, Orthodox Christian Americans feel the impact of drug abuse. It may be helpful for us to clarify further how drug abuse is a "spiritually origined disorder;" how its symptoms represents disordered homes, homes that indelibly engrave their pathology onto otherwise normal children, distorting their growth and development. The presence of these disorders and their symptoms is often less clearly visible in the relatively affluent and perhaps the more culturally endowed people in our society. In middle-class America today we are often insulated, or choose to be insulated, from the reality of unharmonious homes. We experience this against a background of material comfort and worldly success, cushioning ourselves until somehow, out of nowhere, a symptom pushes through the facade: divorce, drugs, suicide. In such ways, our comforts may disable us to be aware of the lack of balance and focus in our lives as well as the deficient quality of our spiritual values.

Confused Models of Faith

When young celebrities and athletes crumble from cocaine overdose or are disqualified from the Olympics due to their use of steroids, we feel disappointment. We might think that the plight of John Belushi, Elvis Presley, and Marilyn Monroe would have an inhibiting effect on other young users of drugs and perhaps some not-so-young as well. But in modern society, we must acknowledge that entertainers have replaced the saints as models for faith, and these models are often confused. How is religion characterized in popular culture? Not only by gross distortion as in songs by people like the popular Madonna, but by omission. Even American history textbooks neglect to present religious values adequately. The religious reasons and the ethical values for the settlement of America by Spanish,

English, and French explorers, and the role religion played in the lives of European immigrants when they settled in the United States, are often never explained. Religious motivation is downplayed. Puritanism is often presented only as the cause of the Salem witch trials of the 17th century, an unmomentous event of a dark movement in New England on which modern-day merchants capitalize. Major events, however, go unacknowledged. The religious beliefs that sustained many leaders and participants in the civil rights movement of the fifties and sixties are rarely mentioned. The religious significance of Thanksgiving is ignored. In one text, for instance, I recall reading that the Pilgrims who began the tradition of a special day for thanking God are described simply as "people." A student could quite understandably dissociate faith from a mere "holiday," seen as just another day off from school. The message of the link between "holy" and "day" has been lost.

Where do people turn? What is the role of home and religion in substance abuse?

Case Study

To illustrate the problem of dysfunctional religion and of dysfunctional homes, I will refer to a teenager, who I will call Peter, whom I counseled while he was in prison. Peter was a healthy, white, 19-year-old, who came from a religious family. He was described in the prison record as an "argumentative, aggressive, 'rock 'n roll' beach comber." His crimes were assault and battery, robbery, and possession of illegal drugs.

Peter described his parents as having a good relationship with each other, but he described his relationship with either of them in stark contrast. He presented himself as basically viewed as a worker on a reinforcement schedule. He explained how his father literally engineered Peter's life with tokens for accomplishments and demerits for errors.

As Peter developed rapport, he shared how the rigidity of his daily management paralleled the stoic religious customs and spirit in the home. Although a "B" to "A" student, Peter's father insisted on "A"s and, while Peter was in high school, his father intensified control.

Without an opportunity for experiencing relationships at home, Peter felt failure and began to act out. In the Roman Catholic high school that he attended, he told the nuns that his parents practiced witchcraft-- and this created an awful stir. The pranks continued, as Peter and his parents became more and more distanced.

At one point, Peter, with some of his other 15-year-old buddies, drove his father's care off without permission or a license. His father was outraged and had Peter brought to a juvenile facility.

When Peter appeared before the judge, he was ordered on probation and reprimanded. Peter's father, however, was not satisfied. He convinced the judge to place Peter in a Boy's home. From then Peter's crime escalated.

Peter told me, "I have anger and resentment for my parents." There was no bonding. He said, "The Church is a rip-off; it's said best in the song 'The Legend Messiah' by the acid rock band Metalica:"

A time for lust

A time for lies

A time to kiss yourself good-bye.

Send me your money

Send me your green

Heaven you will meet.

Make a contribution

As you'll get better

Bow down to the leopard Messiah

Peter's experience of religion was empty. He told me that what is not important to him was "religion, family, and society." What is important is "happiness, honesty and reaching."

It is quite interesting that what might provide Peter's fulfillment, he sees as diametrically opposed to his interests. Are not religion, family and society suppose to offer happiness, honesty and reaching?

Peter told me that his search for meaning was unsuccessful so far through sex, drugs, and rock 'n roll but he is still searching.

To be sure, people who have do not steal. Peter missed the moments which teach one how to search.

Religion and Spirituality

Religion can make a difference. But just as families can be dysfunctional, so can churches and religions. Is our religion functional or dysfunctional?

The Greek word for community, *koinotoita*, literally means communication. Oral communication can be the substance of love. One of the greatest diabolical methods which attacks the family is poor communication: husband against wife, father against son, brother and sister against one another. The family, like the Church, must be a community with common unity. Christian communication and intimacy and love cannot be separate from the love of God, as it is God who models and fuels good relationships. Such family spirituality requires that we pray and talk about our relationship with God. One Christian family I know employs the model of open prayer at the end of each day. If the husband and wife are arguing, they bring the disorder to prayer, because above all else, they agree to pray together. In this way, their closed system of arguments is broken by their commitment to God through communication, the love they experience through God. Love means that we spend such quality time with one another which is more important than making more money to spend on one another. St. Paul insists "love is long suffering, love is kind; love is not self-seeking, it is humble and is not puffed up. But it rejoices in the truth. It bears all things, believes all things, hopes all things, endures all things."

One test of the spiritual vitality of our homes may be answered by one direct question: Very simply, what do I believe? I offer the suggestion that the spiritual factor may be the true treatment of choice in substance abuse, but we need to be clear about spiritual meanings. It is much more than the organization of religion.

References

Barnes, Edward (1990). Children of the damned. *Life*, Volume 13, No. 8.
    New York City: Time Warner.
Merck Sharp (1982). *The Merek Manual*. Fourteenth Editon. Rockway,
    New Jersey: Merck Sharp Laboratories, pp. 1413-1415.

Taking Responsibility for Evil: Addiction and Usury in the Light of Repentance

James R. Campbell

Repentance is not unique to Christianity, but it is uniquely crucial to the formation of a Christian character and way of life. Repentance is neither a virtue nor a duty, yet it becomes both during a Christian formation of the religious self. Perhaps this is so because Christianity begins with the reality of sin and our need to renounce evil. The kerygmatic call to "Repent, for the Kingdom of Heaven is at hand" (Mt. 4:17 RSV) is a call to take responsibility for personal and social evils, as well as a compassionate offer of forgiveness for our sins. But the mystery of repentance is also a kind of light, an illumination of the self that progressively redefines the limits of responsibility and gives compassion a new place in our lives. To see how this happens in modern times and in relation to the contemporary evils of addiction and usury is the burden of this section.

Responsibility and Repentance

So far as I can see, becoming a self involves taking responsibility for oneself. Not total responsibility, but one whose limits are often difficult to determine. When evil is defined formally (as the condition of the possibility of evils) it necessarily accompanies each and all evils, making responsibility for certain evils also bear the burden of having (once again) brought evil into the world. Yet evil also enters the world through evils for which the self is not at all responsible. Suffering and death are surely evils, yet we are not always responsible for their occurrence. What happens to us is often just that: something that happens regardless of our ethical condition. Not only is this true of natural evils, but it also pertains to our experience of evils such as anomie and despair, or affliction and violence. Here, evil is ambiguously located. It happens to us because of the way the human condition itself is burdened by a tradition of such evils, yet we also commonly experience its presence in us as a personal failure. So in what sense can the self truly take responsibility for such evils?

Precisely because attribution of responsibility is ambiguous for evils that straddle the social boundaries of the self, any self that appropriates for itself the reality of such evil redefines the limits of responsibility. The new criteria that come into play when responsibility is clarified of its ambiguity are, I believe, inescapably religious in nature.

We might tentatively describe a religious appropriation of responsibility as one which flows from neither virtue nor duty, but out of a direct desire for the good as such. Whether the good is thought of as a 'who' or not, the relation is personal in nature and constitutive of the self as a spiritual being. The relation of desire to the transcendent is itself religious as well as personal, so the self it posits is also a religious self.[1] That is, a desire for the good posits a self that is more than the totality of its intentional relations because it can never grasp the object of its desire. Having an awareness of its desire for the good, the self becomes a mystery to itself, and its responsible relations in the world become religiously conditioned.

But it is not only the limits of responsibility that are changed by a religious formation of the self. The concept itself comes to have a different meaning. For religious responsibility flourishes only within a life whose origin is repentance and whose consummation is sanctity. Further, responsibility does not comprise the whole field of that life, but finds its exterior always in relation to the interiority of compassion. Both compassion and responsibility are marks of the life of faith, and each is equally grounded in the self's initial movement of repentance.

Repentance is one possible response of a self formed by an ethos with a responsible self as the end in view, but a response that arises only in particular situations. Responsibility may itself become a virtue or a duty for any and all ethical subjects, but repentance resists such universalization. It is a religious, rather than an ethical response; and it, in fact, arises only when and where responsible action has become virtually impossible. Even more concretely, repentance is a response to the domination of the responsible self by evil; and for this reason it, rather than sheer responsiveness, is the root of religious responsibility.

This becomes clearer when we look at the movement of turning from evil to the good which constitutes repentance. The self that is afflicted or in despair is fully subject to the power of evil: its will is said to be in bondage to evil. Yet there is also something within evil itself, something within the workings of affliction and despair that actually opens the door to repentance. This something takes the form of an emptiness of desire. That is, affliction is tied to violence by a dynamic of incessant repetitions and inversions, and so too is despair tied to dread and defiance. But it is possible for excess to exhaust itself, and this moment of stillness is like a wedge in the hands of repentance.

At this point of exhaustion there is an implicit recognition of the finality of the human will, and so a tentative turn toward the infinite as the real ground of freedom. In this moment of hesitancy, freedom is recognized as a good which is absent; affliction and despair are recognized as evil, and as fully present in some particular subjective and historical reality.

The turning away from evil, however, happens as though in a void far from any awareness of desire for the good, and it is only there that the seed forms of repentance germinate. Before the self can really say 'No' to evil and 'Yes' to the good, a momentary exhaustion of repetition moves it to say 'Not now' and 'What if?' Here, the desire of evil for more of itself falls into abeyance and a vague desire for something other than evil opens the door to a direct desire for the good. This direct desire is the fullness of repentance; and the turning itself, the archetype of all free response.

In one sense responsiveness is a condition for the possibility of repentance,[2] but in another sense it is an impediment to the stillness repentance needs as its immediate foundation. Affliction, being a condition of despair over degradation, perpetuates itself by repeatedly evoking despair, by exacerbating responsiveness to sufferings obsessively defined as both degrading and justified (Weil, 1977). It is precisely the exhaustion of this sort of crippled responsiveness that allows the free response of repentance to break the hold of despair on the self.

Moreover, quite ordinary responsiveness may become an impediment to desire for the good when it is fascinated by the fundamental sameness of all immediacy.   Within immediacy, otherness is apprehended through dread; and dread routinely constitutes itself as a temptation to despair unless it can be appropriated by the self through a dialectical response of faith.[3] But once again, the dialectics of faith presuppose a reflexive self formed by an ethos; and when such a self loses itself in immediacy it is only an abeyance of its narcissistic responsiveness that lets repentance posit a new and responsible self.

Yet repentance is both an acceptance of responsibility for oneself and an act of compassion for oneself. It is therefore the foundation of compassion for others; and by means of compassion it moves the self to take responsibility for evils that are ethically problematic.

Addiction and Usury

What is strikingly different about the evils of addiction is that it is currently acknowledged to be a real social and ethical problem whereas the common practice of charging interest on the loan of money is not acknowledged as being in fact usury. Interest on money is legitimated by the dominant bourgeois ethos on various practical and theoretical grounds, with the result that 'usury' is now taken to mean only 'excessive interest.' The evil of usury is apparently condemned, but its basic principle is nonetheless legitimated. As "interest," usury is no longer an evil to be endured if it cannot be avoided, but purportedly a beneficial practice that becomes harmful only when carried to excess. Thus, usury is implicitly compared to a typical vice of excess like drunkenness.

But when drunkenness is redefined as a symptom of the addictive disease process of alcoholism, the comparison backfires. If it is not excessive but rather compulsive intoxication that is wrong, then it is mandatory rather than excessive interest that is unconscionable. Nothing follows from this reversal, of course, except a suspicion that usury may not be a vice of excess, but a real injustice, or even an affliction.

Whether or not that suspicion is correct, the bourgeois legitimation of usury is clearly contrary to the religious ethos out of which it grew. The medieval Western Church condemned usury as being both an injustice and an act of disobedience: it was seen as an affliction of the soul as well as of civil society (LeGoff, 1988). Yet the bourgeois ethos prevailed, not by confrontation, but by changing the meaning of the words "interest" and "usury." This tactic arouses a further suspicion that usury is in fact an evil which is no longer acknowledged as such, and that its real effects on persons and communities are being denied or blamed on something else, just as the effects of alcoholism were ignored or misdiagnosed until very recently.

After almost two generations of study, it is now becoming clear how pervasive and deeply rooted alcoholism is in the (originally bourgeois) culture of modernity. The psychological dynamics of grandiosity and depression that characterize alcoholics are fundamentally the same as those that often afflict their non-alcoholic children. These distinctive actions and attitudes are so pervasive that in some respects it makes perfect sense to speak of ours as an addictive society.[4] But in doing so, we may be ignoring the fact that ours is also a usurious society, and mistaking the effects of usury for those of addiction.

From the point of view of recovery, every addiction is an affliction that is rooted in shame and despair. So despite its new status as a disease, alcoholism remains an affliction from which most recover only through repentance.[5] Calling alcoholism a "disease" is often simply a way of saying that it is the actions and attitudes of the practicing alcoholic that are blameworthy, not the alcoholic as a person. Thus, the disease concept does not in practice absolve the drunk of responsibility or deny the efficacy of repentance. Rather, it facilitates repentance by affirming that alcoholism really is an affliction and that recovery is really possible.

Much of what is known about the process of recovery from alcoholism comes, directly or indirectly, from the experience of alcoholics who have found continuing sobriety in the fellowship of Alcoholics Anonymous.[6] What is most obvious about the Alcoholics Anonymous recovery practice is that it is a spiritual program. That is, it approaches the mental, physical, and emotional aspects of the disease of alcoholism from a spiritual viewpoint for which the experience of repentance is crucial. For what is spoken of in AA as "hitting bottom" is nothing more nor less than the reality of repentance, though often without explicitly religious trappings.

Defined as a turning to the good which begins the life of recovery, repentance is truly the foundation of sobriety. Being a spiritual event, such repentance also leads to a life in which recovery is based on the spiritual discipline known as "working the program." The discipline of recovery is a spiritual one not only because of its reliance on prayer, but also because its object is the formation of a spiritual self on the new foundation given it by the turn away from addiction fundamentally constituted by its letting go of narcissistic projects, of which drinking is only one.

What is apparently a narcissistic self-absorption is, however, often a symptom of deprivation.[7] For the affliction known as alcoholism is one which destroys whatever sense of self the prevailing social ethos may have instilled, and thereby makes it virtually impossible for the alcoholic actually to posit a self in the face of any real otherness. Lacking a stable sense of self from which to begin the spiritual work of becoming a self, the life of an alcoholic is in bondage to compulsivity and lost in sheer immediacy.

Looked at synoptically, the basic features of alcoholism are its movement from shame to despair through the defense of grandiosity, and the way compulsivity continually shames the self. The relation of these two features is that of an affliction to the violence that perpetuates it. So, understandably, the turn to sobriety affected by repentance is also dialectically constituted. Compassion for the afflictions of shame and despair is justified only as responsibility is taken for the violence of compulsive defiance of the good. Together, compassion and responsibility continue the work begun by repentance, the work of becoming a self that constitutes itself as desiring the good.

The human drama of alcoholism and recovery necessarily takes place within a social context that is saturated with affliction. Not only is there a milieu of shame within the alcoholic family, but there is also a widespread cultural ethos of narcissistic immediacy. Self-absorption, or rather the absorption of the self by its compulsions, manifests itself in various ways. It lies at the heart of common similacrum of the work ethic just as surely as it flaunts itself in conspicuous consumption or drunken comportment.

Generally speaking, narcissism denotes being deprived of the chance of developing a mature self. What locks the self into narcissistic immediacy, however, is not the stress or monotony of work, but the reduction of its every action to a cash value. After language, money may well be the one tool that is most versatile and useful for human society,[8] yet the sheer immediacy of its power over social goods makes it quite dangerous as well. There is a real present danger that the self may become lost in the immediacies of money and so fail to become anything more than an infantile version of some common cultural stereotype.

In market economy, the immediacy of money is a function of the range of goods it commands. Hence, the creation of a market of money itself exponentially intensifies its immediacy. But immediacy itself is not always an affliction, and usury and afflicts us with the sheer immediacy of money only because it also degrades us. As I see it, whoever borrows money at interest is degraded by the way in which interest payments prolong being in debt; whoever sells money is degraded by the injustice of the transaction. Yet what I call "systematic usury" is no longer commonly acknowledged to be an evil.

The historical arguments for and against the legitimation of usury turn on three points: 1) What is the nature of money? 2) Does scripture condone usury? 3) Is systematic usury necessary for a free market economy? On all three counts it is the dominant position which mystifies, and marginalized ones that make sense. For example, apologists for the right of creditors to interest payments assert that money is like a tool that can be rented. But what other tool *increases* its market value by being used?[9] Or, if scripture condones charging moderate interest for the loan of money, why are we clearly exhorted to "Lend freely, expecting nothing in return" (Lk. 6:35 RSV)? Pope Urban III (1185-87) did not consider this a 'counsel of perfection' intended only for monks, so why should Calvin's appeal to expediency be allowed to blunt its force?[10] And finally, the fact that free market economies in Western Europe developed within a capitalist system based on systematic usury does not *prove* that free markets require a market in money in order to flourish. Is it not just as plausible to assert that 'free markets' linked to systematic usury habitually fall short of their potential because interest is really a parasitic drag upon the economy?[11] In short, there are too many uncertainties about the legitimacy of systematic usury not to look more closely into how its presence as an unacknowledged evil in our society might relate to afflictions of immediacy.

As credit transactions based on systematic usury become commonplace, the exchange value of money is dominated by its sign value, (Baudrillard, 1988) and the immediacy of possession promised by cash becomes an immediacy isolated from the reality of exchange relations. To exchange is to sacrifice something for the sake of acquiring something else, and money introduces a first disjunction between the sacrifice of value in labor and its acquisition as goods. Credit then introduces another by separating the moment of acquisition from the moment cash value is given in exchange for the goods. This second disjunction heightens the power of immediacy over the moment of acquisition because it hides the social reality of market exchange. In such a social milieu the self is easily afflicted by acquisivity and falls into bondage to its own ignorance of what it is to be and to become a self that is *not* defined by its power to possess goods.

But if money is the social reality of that power, systematic usury is the social foundation for the affliction of acquisitivity. For usury first intensifies the immediacy of money by using a small sum to leverage a great one, and then posits that new immediacy as productivity. This conflates the acquisition of interest money with the production of new social wealth, and posits circulation itself as a source of value. Getting is thereby confused with doing, and money itself becomes acquisitive: it tries to buy the immediacy it embodies just as the acquisitive self tries to possess its own value outside itself in symbolic objects.

The acquisivity of money devoted to usury is, of course, only potential until it is embodied in social relations. But when it is, the fundamental relations of work and property encompass the self with the temptation of regression into immediacy. To begin with, the actuality of usury falsifies the nature of work by the magical way it seems to produce wealth. For money offers no resistance to itself: the reluctance of money to circulate is not a resistance overcome by money itself, but by the need and desire for real productivity. Usury mystifies this relationship by saying that money "works" for us, while it, in fact, does nothing but follow the path of least resistance. Behind its mystique of efficacy, however, the reality of usury is founded on a deliberate avoidance of work and of risk.

At the origins of usury there lies a will to withhold wealth from productive uses unless and until no vestige of risk exists. Usury pretends that it is justified by the risk of loss the lender accepts, but that risk is actually overcome by the collateral the borrower pledges.[12] Interest on loans is, then, virtually extorted from others by their own need and desire to be productive; and systematic usury establishes itself on this foundation of passive violence. It posits scarcity where the social reality is a withholding of wealth, and it thereby insinuates a dread of being 'one too many' into the entire society.[13] Both lender and borrower are then tempted (by dread of this negation) to despair of being a self in the fullest sense; so the one may well become servile and full of resentments, while the other's domination becomes ever more capriciously violent. In either case, the heightened immediacy of money based on usury offers an escape from the afflictions of a milieu of scarcity founded upon the practice of usury. The escape, unfortunately, is only into another form of affliction; namely, acquisivity. And, being a form of compulsive immediacy, acquisivity deprives the self of the energy and detachment it needs to reflect and work on itself.

Narcissistic immediacy is a labile condition in which acquisivity and addictive compulsions are not clearly differentiated. Thus, each implicates the other: compulsivity is acquisitive and acquisivity is compulsive. In a social milieu permeated by usury, the discipline of work whereby effort is deliberately and persistently directed toward overcoming resistances is forgotten. Without knowledge of what it is to work in this fashion, the self finds itself in bondage to its ignorance. For the work of becoming a self is truly work; and a self whose will is ignorant of what it is to work can not of itself carry off the work of positing itself as a real self.[14] So it posits an imaginary self that can not, however, withstand the dread that tempts it into a despairing turn to immediacy.

It is common experience that repentance is what finally frees the self from addiction. But it is not yet common for that same movement of repentance to culminate in the renunciation of acquisivity. Because the modern practice of systematic usury is commonly legitimated by the very wealth it amasses, it freely perpetuates itself through the immediacies, addictive as well as acquisitive, which permeate our culture. It is, however, inevitable that as the spiritual work begun in repentance continues it will integrate more and more facets of culture and life into its new sense of compassionate responsibility. For an alcoholic, sobriety is a way of life that demands honesty and humility, and it is only by working on being honest and humble that sobriety becomes an unshakeable serenity. But it is difficult to be honest and humble while still directly participating in the acquisitive dynamics of usury. So recovery itself entails a certain detachment from the common ethos of acquisivity, and it eventually comes to see usury as one of the cultural correlates of addiction.[15] Thus, the inner dialectic of repentance at work in recovery inevitably demystifies usury; and thereby implicitly takes responsibility for an unacknowledged and anonymous tradition of evil.

Evil in the Light of Repentance

From the standpoint of repentance and recovery, the evil embodied in afflictions of immediacy has a dual nature. Its logic is that of ignorance and mystification; its power is that of a disease or bondage of the will. Recovery from any affliction of immediacy calls for both compassion and responsibility, yet the root response remains repentance, for it is repentance that continues to unify the self in the face of complex and manifold evils such as addiction and usury.

In addiction, for example, the logic of narcissistic deprivation is experienced as a shame for which compassion is the only adequate response. But the compulsive abandonment to immediacy which perpetuates this shame is stilled only by a disciplined working out of the limits of personal responsibility for one's own affliction. In the case of usury, however, the narcissistic immediacy of acquisivity, deeply rooted in dread, is the first object of compassion; while it is the forces of mystification and violence embodied in systematic usury for which responsibility answers. Because compassion and responsibility are thus mutually implicated, taking responsibility for evil means first of all undertaking the work of becoming a compassionate self, and by means of that work, to break the invisible chains of affliction.

Still, the one facet of evil that does not seem to be vulnerable to this spiritual work is its malevolence. That evil desires itself, or desires to be hostile to the good, is what constitutes the reality of malevolence and of radical evil. Since evil is an ignorance and an impotence, it is fitting that its being culminate in a desire that is null.[16] That is, malevolence is a desire for what cannot *be* in any real sense and therefore for what can not ever become reconciled to the good. Yet even what cannot be taken up into the everlasting good while it still desires to be evil can nonetheless be seized by the good.

What appears to happen when evil is touched by the divine energies of good is that it 'repents' of desire for itself, becomes forgetful and hesitant, and falls into conflict with its continuing power for evil. For it is neither the power nor the identity of evil which is changed without human participation, but only its desire; yet desire is a personal relation mediating between different beings. The divine action upon evil is therefore given to us as being analogous to our repentance. In laying the foundation for the possibility of human repentance, evil is seized by a transcendent movement of repentance and reconstituted as an implicit desire, a nostalgia, for the good. Both responsibility and compassion are at work here, since evil is not totally abandoned to its nullity and facility by the divine energies of transformation.[17]

Even though it is human repentance that actually transforms and redeems concrete evils, repentance is possible only as a response elicited by the transcendent, and its very possibility is founded upon a mysterious lack of desire at the very core of evil. When repentance does take place, evil has already been thrown off guard by a divinely evoked nostalgia for the good. Only then is evil caught up into the spiritual work of the new self and gradually integrated into the same concrete good it originally nullified. And because this spiritual work originates in repentance, we are also given to understand that taking responsibility for evil is a compassionate act, and that we are fully responsible for being compassionate.

The ethical principles and virtues exemplified by responsibility and compassion are experientially given as being founded on the one unitary movement of repentance. They are given as being a dialectic mediated by desire for the good, and as possible only within the spiritual work of becoming a self. Just as the unity of the self is constituted by a dialectical play of essence, energy and efficacy,[18] so too does a unitary desire for the good unfold into an ethical praxis oriented toward virtue as its end and resting on principles as its ground.

Living within this threefold dialectic, the self finds itself at work on becoming a spiritual self; and also finds itself within a particular tradition of evil. The fullness of its response is a life of faith nourished by repentance. But that fullness becomes concrete only as the self reaches out with compassion for the afflictions of itself and others, and as it takes on its share of responsibility for evils such as addiction and usury that are "always already there."

Notes

[1] What Kierkegaard calls a "positing" of the self before the Eternal is more concretely described by Levinas as a relation of "desire" with an Other. See Soren Kierkegaard, *Fear and Trembling and The Sickness Unto Death* (Princeton: Princeton University Press, 1968) and Emmanuel Levinas, *Totality and Infinity: An Essay in Exteriority* (Pittsburgh: Duquesne University Press, 1969). For a non-theistic discussion of the dialectical formation of the religious self, see Nishida Kitaro, *Last Writings: Nothingness and the Religious Worldview* (Honolulu: University of Hawaii Press, 1987).

[2] It is clear that responsibility is grounded in responsiveness, yet responsiveness needs to be formed by ethical criteria before it becomes responsible for itself. It becomes a virtue to be responsive and a duty to act responsively only after the self has posited itself as an ethical being. In that formative process simple responsiveness becomes conformed to the principle of limitation present in some particular ethos. See H. Richard Niebhur, *The Responsible Self: An Essay in Christian Moral Philosophy* (San Francisco: Harper and Row, Publishers, 1978).

[3] When dread of otherness enters the conscious dialectic of faith it becomes a negation of trust, and is subject to negation by faith. That is, being recognized as a principle of limitation and negation, dread loses its ubiquity and can be placed within the horizon of the self. Once placed, dread is relatively innocuous and can be negated by the response of reaching out to others and to the divine. Reaching out completes the dialectic of faith, but it is possible only because of a foundational relation of the self and the Other through desire for the good. See Soren Kierkegaard, *The Concept of Dread* (Princeton: Princeton University Press, 1967), and Henri Nouwen, *Reaching Out: The Three Movements of the Spiritual Life* (Garden City, NY: Doubleday and Co., 1986).

[4] The pioneering work on this theme is Anne Wilson Schaef's *When Society Becomes an Addict* (San Francisco: Harper and Row, Publisher, 1987).

[5] This is particularly clear in alcoholism, which is a striking case of addiction to a seemingly non-addictive substance. Alcohol is certainly a mood altering agent, but its action is not that of an opiate. Nonetheless, it does appear that the body produces a certain kind of endorphin (THP) in the presence of toxic concentrations of acetaldehyde, the first metabolite of ethanol. Most of the symptoms of a hangover are the result of acetaldehyde, so the absence of an opiate-like endorphin synthesized during hangovers could be the physiological basis for the full-blown withdrawal syndrome many alcoholics undergo when they stop drinking.

But even if the alcoholic becomes addicted to what happens during hangovers rather than to inebriation itself, not everyone who drinks to excess and has hangovers becomes an alcoholic. For this reason most researchers continue to postulate some sort of hereditary factor that places its bearers at risk of becoming alcoholic. Yet recovery from alcoholism remains difficult even after the postulated abnormality of ethanol metabolism has been effectively silenced by total abstinence from alcohol. In short, the reality of addiction to alcohol is more insidious than can be adequately conveyed by our usual (mechanistic) concepts of disease. See John Wallace, *Alcoholism: New Light on the Disease* (Newport, RI: Edgehill Publications, 1985).

6 The best interpretive account of AA is Ernest Kurt's *Not God: A History of Alcoholics Anonymous* (Center City, MN: Hazelden, 1979). An updated edition is now available under the title *AA: The Story* (San Francisco: Harper & Row Publishers, 1988).

7 That is, when legitimate narcissistic needs are frustrated by social degradation, the self abandons itself obsessively to endless and futile surrogates. Even worse, the interior oscillation between grandiosity and depression that absorbs all the energies of the alcoholic is replicated in the child by its continual immersion in a milieu of shame. An adult alcoholic is perhaps rightly ashamed of having lost a sense of self and being deprived of the chance to become a real self. But that shame also becomes an act of violence when it is insinuated into a child's earliest experiences of itself so that it is forced to live out the parental affliction before it can begin to find its own self.

The broad lines of this analysis were first proposed by Alice Miller in *The Drama of the Gifted Child* (New York: Basic Books, Inc. Publishers, 1981), but without direct reference to alcoholism. See also Heinz Kohut, *The Analysis of the Self* (New York: International Universities Press, 1971).

8 For complex analysis of money as an instrument of exchange of sacrificed values, see George Simmel, *The Philosophy of Money* (Boston: Routledge and Kegan Paul, 1978).

9 Money, as venture capital, act both like a tool and like a resource. As a tool, it is a means of productivity whose efficacy varies with the ability of the person wielding it. As a resource, it does not depreciate because of use, but rather increases in value whenever social wealth is augmented by its productive use. The creditor, in yielding use of venture capital to someone else implicitly recognizes that other person's greater ability to wield money as a tool, and anticipates that because of its being used well as a resource, the money loaned (i.e., the principal) will return enhanced in value by the greater amount of real wealth it now represents and commands. Hence 'interest' payments are in fact a gratuity over and above the legitimate interests of the creditor.

The medieval analysis of usury also distinguished between money as tool (agent) and as resource (material). See John T. Noonan, *The Scholastic Analysis of Usury* (Cambridge: Harvard University Press, 1957).

10 To expect *nothing* in return is also to let go of the principal as well as the expectation of interest payments. Hence, the Church's reading of this text as forbidding usury is a distinct softening of its probable intent. Calvin, however, ignores the gospel text altogether, and bases his justification of interest on the Deuteronomic ambivalence about usury. His reasoning seems to be that if usury was condoned in certain cases even then, how much more must it be permissible for us *who have come to rely on it* in all branches of commerce. See Benjamin Nelson, *The Idea of Usury: From Tribal Brotherhood to Universal Otherhood* (Chicago: The University of Chicago Press, 1969).

11 The turning point for the legitimation of systematic usury was (and is) the common belief that without interest free market economies the wealth they generate would be impossible. However, this common idea is false.

First of all, if a market is defined as "free" to the extent that perfect competition among capitals and individuals is in fact *possible*, then the prevalence of subsidies, monopolies, protective tariffs, tax breaks etc. in capitalist market economies surely indicates that these markets are less than perfectly free. And since not every feature of existing 'free market' economies enhances a condition of perfect (or even fair) competition, it is not at all obvious whether interest is a feature that enhances or compromises the freedom of capitalist markets.

Even though no known market is completely free, it is apparent that those in which competition is prevalent are more free than those in which it is absent. Yet competition tends to reduce the margin of surplus value (profit) anyone can realize and still remain competitive in the marketplace. When the possible margin of profit is reduced by the forces of competition to virtually nothing, there is no longer any monetary incentive to move capital, for no venture is returning a substantially greater profit than any other. Lacking a surplus from which to draw interest payments, no prudent capitalist would voluntarily encumber an existing enterprise with costly payments which would make its products less competitive on the market. Thus it is clear that the basic dynamics of market competition act so as to reduce and eventually eliminate the possibility of collecting interest on loans of venture capital.

The basic principle, then, is clear: the more prefect a degree of competition exists in the market, the lower the interest rate will be. This principle is in fact used to regulate and manipulate the market in money. By raising the prime rate small investors are driven from the market and competition is constricted; by lowering it more competing potential creditors are given access to the market. From this relation it would appear that interest is what *prevents* establishment of a truly free market in venture capital.

An apologist for systematic usury might counter by saying that interest is what prevents the market from sinking into a static equilibrium, that the dynamism of a capitalist style market economy is due to the way that interest (i.e., debt) motivates development of productive forces. This is true as far as it goes. But what capitalism in fact establishes are the conditions for a rigid *dis*equilibrium, rather than a dynamic equilibrium in which profits enlarge and develop the market itself, not just some privileged means of production or methods of monopolization. The fact is that unencumbered capital (that is, money on which no interest is owed) circulates more rapidly and is more quickly plowed back into new production than can capital encumbered by systematic usury. Hence, a market which is free of interest is potentially more vital than one which is dominated by the economic interests of the wealthy.

For a description of the rigidities of capitalism, see Robert Heilbronner, *Behind the Veil of Economics: The Worldly Philosophy* (New York: W. W. Norton and Company, 1988); on the inverse relation of interest and competition, see Joseph Schumpeter's classic work, *The Theory of Economic Development: An Inquiry into Profits, Capital, Credit, Interest, and the Business Cycle* (New Brunswick: Transaction Books, 1983) 157-211.

12 Compensation for some further unsecured risk in the form of interest payments does not lessen or eliminate such risk, but in fact makes it more difficult for the debtor to repay the loan and augments the chances of default. Islamic banks, however, which actually *do* risk loss when loaning venture capital, do not find it necessary to charge interest to offset any such unsecured losses. Instead, their direct participation in business ventures financed through *commenda* contracts allows the profits earned to cover any such losses. The continued existence of interest-free banks in a global economy dominated by the practice of systematic usury makes it clear that interest money is desired precisely because it protects the reluctance of the lender to really participate in the work of generating new wealth. That is, systematic usury is actually a way of avoiding the risk of having to work.

For a clear discussion of how Islamic banks avoid usury, see Nabil A. Saleh, *Unlawful Gain and Legitimate Profit in Islamic Law: Riba, Gharar and Islamic Banking* (New York: Cambridge University Press, 1986), pp. 86-114.

13 See the discussion of scarcity in Jean-Paul Sartre, *Critique of Dialectical Reason* (London: NLB, 1976).

14 For a description of the transition from magic to responsibility through work, see Alain (Emile Chartier), *The Gods* (New York: New Directions Publishing Corporation, 1973).

[15] My own suspicions about usury first surfaced in connection with a study of sobriety. See James R. Campbell, *The Foundation of Sobriety* (Chicago: Master's Thesis at Roosevelt University, 1984).

[16] For a full explication of the concept of the "null," see Karl Barth's "God and Nothingness" in *Church Dogmatics, Vol. III* (Edinburgh: T. and T. Clark, 1960), pp. 289-368.

[17] The superjective or personal nature of the divine is implied by the idea of transcendent spiritual 'work' that makes human repentance possible. See Alfred North Whitehead, *Process and Reality: An Essay in Cosmology* (New York: The Free Press, 1978); or Marjorie Hewitt Suchocki, *The End of Evil: Process Eschatology in Historical Context* (Albany: State University of New York Press, 1988).

[18] A three-fold analysis of unique beings resists facile dichotomization of spiritual and material realms, and rescues the concept of dialectic unity from a mechanical repetition of the formula 'thesis, antithesis, synthesis'. For a medieval exemplar, see John the Scot (Johannes Scotus Eriugena), *Periphyseon: On the Division of Nature* (Indianapolis: The Bobbs-Merrill Company, Inc., 1976).

References

Weil, Simone (1977). The love of god and affliction. George Panichas (ed.), *The Simone Weil Reader,* New York: David McKay Company, Inc., pp. 439-468.

LeGoff, Jacques (1988). *Your Money or Your Life: Economy and Religion in the Middle Ages,* New York: Zone Books.

Baudrillard, Jean. For a critique of the political economy of the Sign. *Selected Writings.* Stanford: Stanford University Press, pp. 51-97.

Towards a Recovery-Oriented Church

Lyn Breck

Several years ago, a young Orthodox man approached me to ask if we could talk. He shared his despair, and his feeling that he could not go on. He mentioned in passing that in order to cope over the past ten years, he had relied on Valium. "I have so many wonderful people helping me", he said, "family, friends, my doctor, my therapist, my priest; but something still isn't right." I agreed and suggested that he accept to go for an evaluation. His diagnosis shocked him: Valium dependence. The recommendation was in-patient rehabilitation.

A seminarian was found comatose, lying in his own vomit after a Paschal celebration. In such circumstances, death due to asphyxiation is common. This young man lived to continue his seminary studies and his drinking.

An Orthodox parish was in serious difficulty. It harbored many factions, with much tension and conflict. The bishop, priest, and parishioners met for discussion in the basement of the church, which served as a bar. In this community alcohol was such an acceptable part of parish life that the choir leader could regularly come to rehearsals with a bottle of vodka. No one made the connection between the alcohol abuse and the conflict in the church.

An Orthodox student dropped out of school. She attributed her drop-out to lack of interest. She had been doing lines of cocaine regularly for six months and had lost quite a bit of weight. Her family and fellow parishioners described her as "tired."

At a church picnic, beer on tap was available in unlimited quantities. There was no supervision of the keg, so several teenagers and even some children got drunk. One of the adults was stopped on her way home for DWI (driving while under the influence).

After Holy Saturday liturgy, wine and bread were served as is the custom in our church . . . Non-alcoholic beverages were not available for children or for recovering alcoholics.

These few incidents raise poignant ethical questions about alcohol/drug issues within our Orthodox Church. They reflect harmful, inaccurate views as to what constitutes help, as well as the tendency to ignore and deny reality. This topic addresses the role of the church in regard to drug and alcohol use, abuse, and chemical dependency.

Any consideration of ethical issues must include their social implications. We need, therefore, to explore and clearly identify our beliefs while giving attention to the decisions we make and the actions we implement as a result of those beliefs.

"Though Orthodox Christianity has clear doctrinal positions and a documented history of ethical teachings, its spirit is not dominated by rules and rigid sanctions. Rather compassion of God, love of Christ and the spirit of philanthropy dominate" (Harakas, 1990).

As Orthodox Christians, our ethical convictions are directly linked to anthropology: who we are in relation to God, who calls us to a fellowship of love with Himself for our salvation. Created in the image and likeness of God, we strive to reflect this true image, not simply as individuals, but together in the communion of the Body of Christ. The basis of our ethical teachings is the law of love which Christ gave to us.

Within our culture, as within our churches, we encounter a disfigured image, one marked by fragmentation and rupture rather than the communion to which we are called. Our status as exiles from the Garden of Paradise has left us in a place of alienation, longing for God. Although God, through Christ, has given us a pathway to reconciliation, we continue to seek after false gods, trying to fill up some hole in our souls. For those addicted to alcohol and/or drugs, the chemicals become the "first love."

The word "addict," from the Latin "addicer," means to assign or deliver over as you would a slave or a captured enemy. Those who experience chemical abuse or dependence move away from the freedom Christ offers towards bondage.

The church is obliged to deal with addictive behaviors. We need to affirm the words of Scripture which proclaim that "the truth shall make you free" (Jn 8:32). "Recovery" is about recovering the divine image in which we were created, accepting the divine love we were meant to share. It is about seeking the renewal of our vocation as God's children and acknowledging God's sovereignty in all aspects of our lives. Recovery in this sense is not limited to those affected by drug and alcohol problems. Recovery is meant for all of us as we become healing agents for one another.

When there is chemical abuse or addiction in a family, the other members of the family are negatively affected. They learn to tolerate the intolerable as they attempt to control the behavior of the chemically abusing person. With the progression of the disease, spiritual deterioration occurs, leading to spiritual bankruptcy for all members of the family. This scenario is present in our church families as well.

It was rumored that an ascetic-looking character was recently holding a sign which read: "The end is not near. You must learn to cope!" Learning to cope with drug and alcohol problems in the church requires concerted, informed effort. It clearly requires courage to overcome our denial. This effort, ideally, needs to take place in several areas: education, prevention, intervention, treatment, and aftercare; and it includes ongoing support.

Education/Prevention

Education is an indispensable tool for dealing with addictions. None of the "helpers" of the young man suffering from Valium addiction realized that they were actually enabling him in his disease.

The faculty and staff of our seminaries need education in the area of addictions in order to recognize symptoms of drug and alcohol abuse. Had the faculty been aware of the seriousness of alcohol poisoning, the student found comatose after Easter would have been referred for mandatory evaluation and treatment. Within the context of the seminary curriculum, both through orientation and through courses in Pastoral Theology, seminarians can learn the basics of how to deal with alcohol and drug problems.

Our future priests and lay leaders could have an opportunity within the seminary context to explore their own family backgrounds, in order to relate information about addictive family systems to their own experience. They could identify unhealthy, unspoken rules which foster addictive systems, especially the tendency to keep secrets.

The parish structure, with its course of religious instruction for all ages, offers an exceptional opportunity to include education about drugs and alcohol. Our parishes need to become informed about the profession of mental, physical, emotional and spiritual deterioration through chemical abuse and chemical dependency. Workshops devoted to alcohol and/or drug awareness can be scheduled as church events.

Sources of renewal such as retreats which focus on developing and maintaining a healthy spiritual life, together with supportive networks within the community, contribute to ongoing prevention.

Written and recorded materials can be a source of vital information available to large numbers of Orthodox through the media. Currently our church is in direct need of materials offering drug and alcohol information from an Orthodox perspective.

A crucial aspect of prevention is the development of alcohol/drug policies that encourage a healthy relationship with chemicals. Examples of policies to consider include: 1) establishing the church as a drug-free zone, making an explicit statement that minors will not be served, and 2) providing supervision which enforces this policy, 3) formulating a policy in regard to the presence of bars in churches (my own conviction is that bars do not belong there at all), and 4) hosting alcohol-free events where people can learn to enjoy themselves without relying on chemicals.

Intervention

Intervention refers to a method of offering help to a chemically-abusing or chemically-dependent person. It requires the competence of a professional who meets with the concerned individuals in planning the intervention. It is important that we identify professionals skilled in this area and learn to collaborate with them. It is, of course, equally important that we learn how to identify those who need intervention.

Treatment

Employee and Student Assistance Programs provide help for individuals who face a variety of problems including drug and alcohol abuse. Clergy and their families are not exempt from such problems, and they need confidential, competent assistance available to them. For the most part, our churches are not providing this service. There is, however, one orthodox seminary where such a program is currently in effect for faculty, staff, students, and their families, and it has proved highly beneficial.

Referral resources for each specific geographical area need to be developed. What are the appropriate treatment resources? What is the possibility of collaboration between alcohol and drug professionals and pastors and/or lay groups concerned with this problem?

Aftercare/Ongoing Support

Parishes can consider visiting/outreach programs to offer support to families affected by drug and alcohol problems. A major barrier getting help for chemically-dependent persons and their families is shame. They often retreat into isolation and silence because of the stigma attached to addiction. Active reaching out by trained parishioners in attempts to break the silence can offer an invaluable witness of love and fellowship.

Our churches can also provide hospitality to Twelve-Step Programs. Some Orthodox Churches have developed Twelve-Step Programs of their own, which have met with a supportive welcome and positive results. The Twelve-Step Programs based on spirituality allow participants to receive and offer support as they share with one another their experience, strength, and hope.

Priests can form pastor-to-pastor support groups and meet on a regular basis to share how they deal with alcohol/drug problems in their parishes or in their own lives. A large proportion of our Orthodox pastors have grown up in alcoholic homes. Without realizing it, they are still using survival strategies adopted in childhood to deal with alcohol and drug problems in their church communities.

Ministry

Ministry to alcoholics, drug addicts, and their families is not solely the responsibility of clergy. It is a function of the entire church community, and evolves out of a concern for communicating the Gospel and living out that Gospel in the context of salvation and reconciliation (Cairns, p. 8).

Thomas Cairns, in his book *Preparing Your Church For Ministry to Alcoholics and Their Families*, sets some minimal criteria for this ministry. These criteria are applicable as well to families facing drug addiction.

The first and most basic component is that any ministry to this population be motivated by love and desire to help. Cairns maintains that this ministry needs to be an active outreach by those who are alert to the specific symptoms of the disease, and who know how to offer help appropriately, including spiritual guidance. He insists that this work be a permanent part of church service, and that the pastor, staff, and lay team be trained to deal with problems of this nature. As a basis for this ministry, an adequate survey of the needs of the church community is essential (Cairns, pp. 43-54).

As we work towards viable solutions to drug and alcohol problems within the church, we need to be aware that God's plan is precisely to use broken people . . . That includes each one of us. As a part of our healing journey, all of us need to give up our attempts to be moral perfectionists, those who are always "right." We also need to give up our attempts to be relational perfectionists, those who are always "loving." We need, in other words, to be in touch with our brokenness.

In the passage from Luke 4:18-21, Christ enters the temple of his hometown, Nazareth, and stands to read the passage from Isaiah which proclaims:

> The Spirit of the Lord is upon me, because He has anointed me to preach the gospel to the poor. He has sent me to heal the brokenhearted, to preach deliverance to the captives, to set at liberty those who are oppressed, and to proclaim the acceptable year of the Lord.

For just such people, Christ came. As He finished reading, He handed the scroll back to the attendant, took his place and said: "Today this scripture has been fulfilled in your hearing."

So let us acknowledge our brokenness. Let us acclaim Christ as healer, and use our gifts and talents wisely as we become His co-workers, to bring healing to our own hearts, to our families and to our church communities. By God's grace, may we come to accept the challenging and difficult task of becoming a "recovery-oriented church."

References

Cairns, Thomas. *Preparing Your Church for Ministry to Alcoholics and Their Families,* Springfield, IL: Charles C. Thomas, 1986, p.8, pp. 43-54.
Harakas, Stanley S. *Health and Medicine in the Eastern Orthodox Tradition,* New York: Crossroad, 1990, p.18.

About the Editor

JOHN T. CHIRBAN, Ph.D., Th.D., is Professor of Psychology and Co-Director of Counseling and Spiritual Development at Hellenic College and Holy Cross School of Theology in Brookline, Massachusetts. He is an Advanced Fellow in Behavioral Medicine at Harvard Medical School at the Cambridge Hospital, and Director of Cambridge Counseling Associates in Cambridge, Massachusetts.

Among Dr. Chirban's recent writings are (editor and contributor) *Health and Faith: Medical, Psychological and Religious Dimensions* (Lanham, Maryland: University Press of America, 1991); *The Interactive-Relational Approach to Interviewing: Encountering Lucille Ball and B. F. Skinner* (Ann Arbor, Michigan: University Microfilms International, 1991); (editor and contributor) *Healing: Interdisciplinary Perspectives in Medicine, Psychology, and Religion* (Brookline, Massachusetts: Holy Cross Press, 1991).

CONTRIBUTORS

John Breck, Th.D. is associate professor of New Testament and Ethics at St. Vladimir's School of Theology. He is Editor of the *St. Vladimir's Quarterly.*

James Campbell, M.A. studied theology at the University of Chicago.

John T. Chirban, Ph.D., Th.D., serves as professor of psychology and co-director of Counseling and Spiritual Development at Hellenic College/Holy Cross School of Theology and is an advanced fellow in behavioral medicine at Harvard Medical School at The Cambridge Hospital.

Sharon Chirban, Ph.D. is a clinical fellow in psychology at Harvard Medical School at The Cambridge Hospital.

John Demakis, M.D. is professor of clinical medicine at Stritch School of Medicine, Loyola University, in Maywood, Illinois. He is director of the Midwest Center for Health Services and Policy Research at the Veteran's Administration Hospital in Hines, Illinois.

Demetrios Demopulos, Ph.D. is a geneticist who has completed studies in preparation for ordination to the priesthood at Holy Cross School of Theology.

Vigen Guroian, Ph.D. is professor of religion at Loyola College in Maryland.

Monk Ioannikios is a monk at the Skete of the Prophet Elias in Mount Athos, Greece.

Martin Marty, Ph.D. is professor of religion at the University of Chicago. He serves as editor of the *Christian Century*.

William F. May, Ph.D. is professor of ethics at Southern Methodist University.

Frank J. Papatheofanis, Ph.D., M.D., is assistant professor and director of the biomaterials and bioengineering laboratory of the Department of Orthopaedics for the University of Illinois.